50 Ways to Love Your Daughter

Approaching the Heart with a Rational Mind

Sarah Cline, Ph.D.

Copyright © 2023 Sarah Cline, Ph.D.

All rights reserved.

The contents of this book may not be reproduced, duplicated, or transmitted without direct written permission from the author.

Under no circumstances will any legal responsibility or blame be held against the publisher for any reparation, damages, or monetary loss due to the information herein, either directly or indirectly.

Legal Notice:

This book is copyright-protected. This is only for personal use. You cannot amend, distribute, sell, use, quote, or paraphrase any part of the content within this book without the consent of the author.

Disclaimer Notice:

Please note the information contained within this document is for educational and entertainment purposes only. Every attempt has been made to provide accurate, up-to-date, and reliable complete information. No warranties of any kind are expressed or implied. Readers acknowledge that the author is not engaging in the rendering of legal, financial, medical, or professional advice. The content of this book has been derived from various sources. Please consult a licensed professional before attempting any techniques outlined in this book.

By reading this document, the reader agrees that under no circumstances is the author responsible for any losses, direct or indirect, which are incurred as a result of the use of the information contained within this document, including, but not limited to, errors, omissions, or inaccuracies.

ISBN: 978-1-937209-26-1

Contents

	Introduction	1
1.	Understanding Personality Types: A Deep Dive	4
2.	Communication Is Key	19
3.	Emotional Closeness	35
4.	Proper Socialization	59
5.	A Quest for Balance	79
6.	Establishing Healthy Boundaries	92
7.	Have Fun	103
8.	Final Thoughts	121

Introduction

Welcome to *50 Ways to Love Your Daughter*. If you've picked up this book, you are most likely a parent, eager to enhance your relationship with your daughter, or perhaps you're just gearing up for what the future holds for your little bundle of joy—or bundle-of-joy-to-be.

Whatever the case, you've taken a significant step toward deeper understanding and connection—so, congratulations are in order.

Throughout this volume and larger series, we'll focus on three universal personality categories: the reserved Cave Dweller (CD), the outgoing Mountain Yeller (MY), and the Straddler, who exhibits mixed traits. Recognizing and understanding these types is crucial, as they shape relationship dynamics in untold ways. Our aim is to provide practical insights into fundamental personalities, ensuring you're better equipped to navigate and strengthen your relationships. What's more, you'll walk away with a better grasp of who *you* truly are—and by knowing yourself, you're better for others.

Armed with the insights from this book, you'll not only interpret actions but also understand the deeper motivations behind them with greater ease. Prepare to see your daughter—and perhaps yourself—in a whole new light...

The Power of Personalities

Ahead, we'll demystify the core attributes of CDs, MYs, and Straddlers, equipping you with insights to comprehend and appreciate the nuances of each type. Appreciating these differences allows you to interpret your daughter's behaviors accurately within her unique personality context, thus avoiding flawed assumptions.

Too often in relationships, you mistakenly attribute conflicts and misunderstandings to a lack of love, empathy, or respect. Yet, more frequently, it's a simple gap in understanding. When you don't perceive the underlying personality traits driving your daughter's actions, you can misinterpret her intentions, leading to undue tension. It's not always about agreeing or having the same viewpoint; it's about acknowledging and respecting these inherent differences. By recognizing the core personality traits of CDs, MYs, and Straddlers, you can better empathize with your daughters, allowing love to fully flourish.

Before We Begin

50 Ways to Love Your Daughter offers no quick fix or casual checklist. Instead, it emphasizes "love" as an active endeavor, demanding both attention and effort. While you'll find a great deal of guidance here, it's up to you to apply these insights authentically.

Engaging with this material will require introspection, and there will be moments that challenge your current understanding of parenting and relationships—and everything else, for that matter. Yet, it's in these times of reflection and adjustment that true growth happens...and, here, the fruits of your labor could scarcely be sweeter—some real incentive.

Through patience and ongoing application, you're not just enhancing a single bond but, rather, refining how you connect. How you live. How you share your soul. So, love the process, love yourself, and love your daughter on a whole new level.

Before we begin, remind yourself: you're a masterpiece—and a work in progress, as is your relationship with your daughter.

Chapter One

Understanding Personality Types: A Deep Dive

Do you find yourself needing help understanding your daughter's personality traits? Are you frustrated that they're so dissimilar to yours? Chances are, when you first met your daughter after she was born, she was a bundle of surprises. You got to meet a new personality and experience her likes and dislikes. But once those years of childhood pass, especially during her teenage years, more times than not, those differences became a source of frustration, misunderstanding, and even strife.

Understanding personality types is an essential piece of the puzzle when seeking to understand your little girl. Appreciating your daughter means discovering their girly layers and complexities, and all of them should garner your attention if you are to experience a happy and healthy relationship.

In this chapter, we will discuss the personality types of the Cave Dweller daughter, which we will refer to as CD, the Mountain Yeller or MY daughter, and the Straddler daughter. Learning about these three basic personality types will give you a clearer picture of the unique benefits and challenges each creates. And understanding is an essential first step to bringing harmony and happiness into your everyday life.

Origins of Personality Types

Before the modern-day classifications of CDs and MYs and even before psychiatrists and psychologists stepped onto the scene, ancient civilizations sought to explain human behavior and its various nuances.

The Ancient Greeks

The ancient Greeks developed the theory of "four humors" to explain the causes of health and illness, both mental and physical. This theory suggested that an individual's temperament was influenced by bodily fluids: blood (sanguine), yellow bile (choleric), black bile (melancholic), and phlegm (phlegmatic). The Greeks thought these humors were directly related to being sanguine (cheerful), choleric (short-tempered), melancholic (reserved), or phlegmatic (relaxed). Therefore, the balance of these humors was believed to influence an individual's temperament, health, and overall disposition. An imbalance of this humor led to behaviors that, today, we associate with certain mental illnesses. For example:

- Sanguine (blood) was associated with cheerful, optimistic, enthusiastic personality traits. An imbalance was thought to be due to a person having too much blood in their body, which would cause them to be overly confident and have impulsive behavior. Possible narcissistic and bipolar disorder.

- Choleric (yellow bile) was associated with being ambitious, passionate, and easily angered. An imbalance causes anger, irritability, or extremely aggressive behavior and rage. Possible borderline personality disorder.

- Melancholic (black bile) was associated with being thoughtful, reflective, and often sad or depressed. This imbalance was associated with melancholy and depression.

- Phlegmatic (phlegm) was associated with being calm, reliable, and often unemotional or apathetic. An imbalance was associated with lethargy, sluggishness, or a lack of motivation, which, much like melancholic excess, is a symptom of depression.

Treating these emotional ailments is where things got even more interesting. If the Greeks thought you had an imbalance of any of these four humors, you would likely have received one of the following treatments:

Dietary Changes: Prescribed depending on the humor in excess. For instance, someone deemed overly choleric might be advised to avoid hot or spicy foods that would "agitate" the yellow bile.

Bloodletting: If you were someone believed to have an excess of sanguine humor, it was common practice to be prescribed bloodletting. This process involved removing blood from the body by way of leeches or actual cutting.

Purging: To remove excess bile or phlegm, laxatives were used, as were emetics, which induced vomiting.

Baths/Sweating: To promote toxin removal, balms and ointments were applied to the skin to help imbalance these four humors.

The Greeks' attempts to "treat" imbalances in personality or health were based on the observations and the knowledge they had at the time. The four humors theory was eventually replaced with more accurate medical models, but its influence can still be seen in some of our languages today.

The Introvert and the Extrovert

Carl Gustav Jung (1875–1961) was a Swiss psychiatrist, psychoanalyst, and the father of analytical psychology. He developed several concepts that had a profound influence on both psychology and popular culture. One of her most notable contributions was the concept of "introversion" and "extraversion" (often used in the more modern manner: introvert and extrovert). Jung's theory asserts that introversion and extraversion are attitudes that represent the direction in which a person's psychic energy flows.

Extraversion (Extrovert)

According to Jung, the extrovert's energy flows outward. This personality type is more oriented toward the external world and derives energy from interacting with its surroundings, including people, events, and situations. If your daughter is an extrovert, she tends to be more outgoing, social, and interested in external events. She is typically action-oriented and more comfortable in social situations than an introverted girl. External factors influence girly extroverts, who are occasionally prone to negative introspection.

Introversion (Introvert)

As the name suggests, the introvert's energy flows inward. This personality type is more oriented toward her inner world, relying on introspection and internal reflection. If your daughter is introverted, she is generally more reserved and often feels more comfortable with individual activities or smaller group settings. She derives energy and pleasure from thinking, daydreaming, or exploring ideas. Although an introverted daughter's daily practices tend to lead to social isolation, she often has a small number of deep connections with people of their choosing.

Jung believed that everyone has an introverted and extroverted side, with one being more dominant than the other. It's a spectrum, and while some girls might be near the extremes of that spectrum, most individuals fall somewhere in between.

Cave Dweller (CD) and Mountain Yeller (MY) Daughters

While not strictly rooted in these historical contexts, the CD and MY classifications are evolved constructs reflecting the same human desire to understand ourselves and others in our world more deeply.

While our contemporary understanding of the CD and MY classifications doesn't stem directly from ancient Greek or Jungian theories, much like their historical counterparts, they are observed patterns in modern relationships. By identifying recurring patterns, you can forge tools to help you navigate and harmonize interpersonal interactions.

Deeper Dive into the Cave Dweller (CD) Daughter

We must first learn about their traits to determine whether you and your daughter fall into the CD or MY category.

Reserved Nature

If your daughter is a CD, she will predominantly be calm and reserved. She is introspective and tends to hold her emotions close to her chest because she values her inner world and the sanctuary it provides. Her reserved nature doesn't mean that she is indifferent or doesn't care about her parent; it just means that she processes her emotions internally and over time.

For instance, after an argument, a CD girl might withdraw to process her feelings rather than immediately confront an issue. A CD daughter does this because she typically feels uncomfortable with strife and needs time to work through her emotions and how to communicate her feelings.

Socially, a CD girl is often found in quieter corners, engaging in deep conversation with one or two individuals rather than in the center of a party. In group discussions, a CD will offer insights only if specifically asked or if she feels strongly about a topic.

Logical Thinking and Literal Communication

A CD daughter leans more toward analytical and logical thinking. She makes decisions only after careful contemplation and weighing the pros and cons. She works hard to keep her emotions from clouding her judgment. This logical thinking manifests in her communication, she will get to the point without inserting emotions or using stories to embellish her point.

For example, if you discuss a film with a CD girl, she will likely dissect plot points with impeccable logic and even point out strengths and weaknesses. But she often misses the emotional undertones of the movie. If you ask a CD if she liked the cake you brought for dessert, she might reply, "Yes," without diving into flowery descriptives.

It's important to note that a CD daughter may also get frustrated with an embellished story that only gets to the point. It doesn't mean she doesn't want to hear the story or doesn't care what the person has to say; her brain is just geared toward immediate outcomes.

Need for Space

A CD daughter has an inherent need for emotional and physical personal space. For her, requiring space is not about distancing herself from loved ones. It's about needing solitude to recharge and reflect.

CD girls enjoy reading books in a cozy nook or going for solitary walks. She may listen to music while cooking dinner instead of talking. This alone time is essential for a CD girl, especially after a day filled with social interactions.

Singular Focus

A CD daughter has unparalleled concentration when engrossed in a task and prefers completing that task to her satisfaction before tackling another.

If you attempt to talk to a CD girl while she's writing an email, for example, she may be so absorbed in what she's writing that you'll be tuned out. It's not that what you're saying is unimportant to her; it's just challenging for her to spread her focus on more than one thing at a time because she gives each item her full attention.

Social Preferences

Traditionally, if your daughter were labeled an introvert, others would consider her antisocial. But that couldn't be farther from the truth. An introvert, or a CD girl, just leans toward more intimate social interactions. Large gatherings can overwhelm a CD girl and drain her mental and emotional battery.

Emotional Processing

While CD daughters might not outwardly express their emotions, they experience them deeply. However, their internal reflections may lead to a delay in their outward emotional expression. While CD daughters may seem distant after an emotional confrontation, they must process the interaction before reacting. A CD girl needs time to contemplate a disagreement, analyze the conversation, and figure out where things went wrong before she can move on to a resolution. This meditation is essential for a CD girl's counterpart to understand; the more they push her to express herself, the more she will clam up in response.

Deeper Dive into the Mountain Yeller (MY) Daughter

If your daughter is an extrovert, chances are she's been called that more than once in her lifetime. Extroverts are typically known for being outgoing and the life of any party. But there's so much more to them than meets the eye.

Outgoing Nature/Group Socialization

A MY girl is inherently outgoing. Her energy thrives on interactions and being around people as often as possible. Instead of needing time alone to recharge, MY girl wants to be out and involved.

At a social event, MY girls will be the first to initiate games and dancing and will often bounce from person to person, catching up rather than focusing on one task at a time. Deep conversations are still on the table, but not at a social event. MY girls usually rally their friends for a group outing over a weekend rather than sitting at home reading a book or watching TV. Even in the workplace, MY daughters love group projects and find collaborative brainstorming and teamwork exciting.

Emotion-Driven

MY girls are heart-ruled because they lead with their intuition and emotions. Being ruled by their heart doesn't mean their decisions are devoid of logic, but their feelings heavily influence their reactions. MY daughters can be emotional during arguments but are also the first to send a heartfelt message to a friend upon hearing they are having a rough time.

An MY girl's emotions will show throughout her storytelling, so be patient when she tells you about an event or relays the plot to a movie. Chances are both will be full of details and embellishments.

Connection and Touch

My daughters crave genuine connections and physical touch—whether a hug, a pat on the back, or simply holding hands.

It reinforces their feeling of being connected. In relating with you, the MY girl will crave physical affection and see it as a top priority over other needs—something we'll discuss in depth a bit later.

Dynamic Focus

The MY daughter is a natural multitasker. Instead of focusing on one task at a time, her attention shifts between assignments. She enjoys the energy she gets from juggling multiple things and often gets bored working on one project for an extended period.

The MY girl doesn't mind dealing with paperwork but works through it while watching television or listening to music. As for conversations, the MY daughter loves to chat, but don't be surprised if you find the MY girl scrolling on her phone while talking with you. It's not that the MY girl thinks what you have to say is unimportant; her mind runs faster, and she's more comfortable processing more than one thing at a time.

Inferential Communication

The MY daughter often communicates using stories, anecdotes, and metaphors rather than getting straight to the point. She relies on indirect implications and expects others to infer meanings, which can confuse some who may need to be more familiar with her communication style.

During an argument, the parent of a MY girl may find it hard to decipher what the MY girl wants, even if she feels she has told them directly. It's essential to have a middle ground where communication is concerned, especially if your girl is an MY trying to get through to a CD. Their communication styles are very different.

Immediate Emotional Expression

Unlike their CD counterparts, MY daughters are quick to express their emotions. They're an open book and rarely hesitate to share their feelings of joy and disappointment. This can be overwhelming for a CD uncomfortable with an emotional display.

One of the greatest fears the MY girl faces is the fear of rejection. If an MY daughter has a CD parent who usually pulls away at any sign of conflict, this can be a bone of contention. The MY girl will take your withdrawal as a sign of personal rejection. It's important to communicate that you are not rejecting her and need time to wrap your head around and process the disagreement. Give the MY daughter verbal and physical affirmations whenever possible.

If you are a CD and your daughter is an MY, don't panic; it doesn't mean you cannot have a successful relationship. There are plenty of amazing and fulfilling relationships between opposites. It just means it will take time, work, and patience to learn one another's needs and effectively communicate.

The Straddler Daughter

If your daughter is a Straddler, she is adaptable and enjoys the best of both worlds. She can immerse herself in a book like a CD girl or be the life of a party like the MY girl. She possesses an emotional agility that allows her to straddle her personality types seamlessly. While this book predominantly focuses on CD and MY daughters, Straddlers can use it to understand the extremes and navigate their middle ground more effectively.

Excellent Balance between Reflection and Expression

A Straddler girl can introspect like a CD, valuing quiet moments of thought. Yet, she also appreciates the expressive vitality of the MY and shares her feelings and ideas openly when a situation calls for it. She is as happy spending a quiet evening reading as attending a book club and actively participating in a lively discussion.

Adaptable in Social Situations

While she might not always be the life of the party, a Straddler daughter easily adjusts to situations based on the social settings and the company involved. She can engage in a one-on-one conversation at a party and then join a group game or be at the party's center later in the evening.

Values Both Logic and Emotion

A Straddler daughter approaches situations with a logical mindset but is equally attuned to the emotional undercurrents, valuing the importance of feelings in decision-making. For example, if a peer faces a personal issue, the Straddler girl will offer practical solutions while providing emotional support.

Flexibility in Needs and Fears

The Straddler daughter's hierarchy of needs will fluctuate based on circumstances, and she might experience fears from the CD's spectrum, such as loss of security and the MY's fear of rejection. However, adaptability allows her to prioritize different aspects of her life. While working on an important school project, she will prioritize educational achievement, but in her downtime, she will focus on friendships and familial connections.

Fluid Communication Styles

A Straddler daughter can communicate directly and inferentially, often adjusting her communication based on the recipient. For example, when conversing with her detail-oriented teacher, she will be direct and to the point, but when she talks to her best friend, she becomes expressive and delves into all the nitty-gritty details.

Straddlers possess an innate ability to mediate and find common ground, especially in relationships where CDs and MYs might find themselves at odds. Her adaptability enables her to comprehend and empathize with both personality types, easing communication and diminishing misunderstandings.

A Straddler may seem like the perfect personality type. However, everyone encounters their share of struggles. The flexibility of a Straddler often confuses her preferences and needs. She might sometimes feel stretched or trapped in the middle, particularly in a polarized situation where she wishes to please her parents or peers and struggles to voice her disagreements. A Straddler daughter must discern what is truly significant to her while learning to navigate her personality type, much like everyone else.

So, How Do You Find Common Ground

I'm a CD, and my daughter is a MY; is my relationship with her doomed?

No! In this book, we don't tell you how to "cope" with your daughter's differences. We allow you to realize each person's unique strengths in a relationship. A CD's introspection can balance a MY's spontaneity. A MY's vivacity and exuberance can harmonize beautifully with a CD's depth and stability.

Recognizing these different traits is merely the first step to a healthy relationship. The real challenge, and indeed the focus of this book, is to find ways to navigate the complexities of these interactions. After all, the beauty of a relationship truly unfolds in the dance between these personalities.

Key Takeaways

Diving into the intricacies of personality types isn't about affixing labels but enriching your understanding. With these insights, you're now armed with the necessary vocabulary to navigate the labyrinth of human emotions and connections, fostering an environment where love thrives, understanding blossoms, and relationships flourish. As you traverse this journey, remember that the goal isn't to change but to adapt, understand, and love more deeply.

The foundation for a nurturing relationship starts with understanding—understanding yourself, your daughter, and the dynamics of your interaction. With the knowledge of CD and MY personality traits, you're well on your way to deepening that understanding, setting the stage for the subsequent chapters that will guide you on how to cherish your daughter in ways that resonate with both of you.

Understanding personality differences is essential for nurturing compatibility. This chapter has illuminated the fundamental traits of CDs, MYs, and Straddlers.

- **Reserved Nature:** Respect your CD daughter's need for personal space and quiet reflection. Don't force immediate emotional reactions.

- **Logical Thinking:** Recognize your CD daughter's analytical approach. Be patient as they process before expressing feelings.

- **Singular Focus:** Acknowledge that multitasking is difficult for your CD daughter. Allow them to complete or pause their task before they give you their full attention.

- **Emotion-Driven:** Empathize with your MY daughter's emotions. Give your girl positive affirmations/compliments and physical affection.

- **Inferential Communication:** Listen for meanings implied indirectly in your MY daughter's stories. Learn to read between the lines.

- **Dynamic Focus:** Accept your MY daughter's wandering attention. Multitasking is her nature. However, if you need her full focus, tell her.

- **Excellent Balance:** Appreciate the adaptability of a Straddler daughter. Avoid putting them in the middle of conflicts.

- **Flexible Needs:** Accommodate shifts in a Straddler daughter's priorities. Reassure her of your unconditional love.

Chapter Two

Communication Is Key

Effective communication is the foundation of any parent-child relationship. It also does not discriminate against personality type.

Communication is the bridge that connects us all—whether you are CDs or MYs. It enables you to come to a mutual understanding and build a stronger bond.

In this chapter, we'll delve into the essential components of communication that can strengthen the bond you have with your daughter. Moreover, we'll navigate the unique traits of each personality type and how you can use personality indicators to validate your daughter and her needs.

While it's easy to be swayed by the idea that love is a mysterious force beyond your control, the reality is that maintaining a lasting relationship requires conscious effort, respect, and a willingness to understand. This journey of appreciation goes beyond knowing your daughter's favorite "things." It's about diving deep into her psyche, comprehending her unique personality traits, and recognizing how her soul-deep attributes interact with yours.

In the age of digital connections and instant gratification, you may sometimes forget the beauty of human interaction. You often overlook the importance of patience, reflection, and presence with your loved ones. Thus, you can pause, reflect, and feel as you progress through this chapter. By fostering an environment of open communication and mutual respect, you're not just building relationships and bonds but cultivating relationships that thrive on understanding, compassion, and genuine connection. Here are some strategies and ground rules to help you convey your emotions effectively:

Express Feelings without Instigating Conflicts

Expressing your feelings is crucial for any relationship, but it's also essential to do so without triggering conflicts. It's too easy to get wrapped up in emotions when expressing them to someone else—especially when you're first sorting through them—so it's crucial to take a step back, breathe, and formulate thoughts before verbalizing them. This is also true with your daughter. Make sure to keep the heightened emotions to a minimum to avoid as much conflict as possible.

Remain Calm

Try not to overreact to difficult situations. If you remain calm, it's more likely that your daughter will feel like she has the space and ability to consider your perspective.

Express Feelings with Words, Not Actions

If you start to get angry and feel you may lose control, take a break and do something to help yourself feel calm.

- Take a walk.
- Do breathing exercises.
- Interact with a pet.
- Journal.
- Read a book.

Address One Issue at a Time

Only introduce tertiary issues once the primary problem has been fully discussed. This way, you'll avoid what experts call the "kitchen sink effect." Dr. John Mordechai Gottman (b. 1942), an American psychologist and professor at the University of Washington, coined the term to describe the act of one person in a discussion or argument throwing "everything but the kitchen sink" into it by dredging up past mistakes and grievances. This tactic is particularly counterproductive, as it's often overwhelming to the person receiving the grievances. This is especially true of your daughter.

Mitigate the Kitchen Sink Effect

When emotions flare up, it's natural to fall back on old disappointments or hurt feelings—especially if they're similar to current difficulties.

One of the most common reasons for someone to resort to "kitchen sinking" is quite simple: to win the argument. However, this amounts to "winning the battle but losing the war." It's a surefire way to sabotage potential progress in your relationship with your daughter, as she will likely feel attacked and be less likely to want to communicate with you going forward.

Poor communication skills can be to blame for this type of behavior. Sometimes, a person doesn't even realize they're being destructive—or that they're exhibiting this behavior at all. This is usually the case for individuals who have never truly learned how to express and work past their feelings healthily. And is quite common in parents who have past traumas.

Let's break that trauma, though. Dredging up past mistakes is almost always counterproductive, and your daughter doesn't need to feel bullied or overwhelmed by an onslaught of criticisms when she's having a discussion with you.

Instead of resorting to this method, remain calm and employ effective communication techniques. You don't want to bully your daughter, no matter how angry you may be. Easier said than done, of course! It's a difficult habit to break, but if you participate in this behavior, the most important thing to do is become aware and remain calm. If you value your relationship with your daughter and want to move forward, choose your words mindfully and let go of past transgressions, no matter how frustrated you are.

Resist Underhandedness

Avoid hitting below the belt or being underhanded. Never use these conversations to attack your daughter—especially in sensitive areas. These attacks only foster distrust, anger, and harmful vulnerability.

You don't want to "win" arguments. You want to work through issues by effectively communicating.

Avoid Clamming Up

Positive results can only be obtained by way of proper communication. It's easy to feel emotionally charged when discussing your feelings with your daughter, especially if they've upset you or you think they're upset with you. When emotions run high, you "clam up" or shut down often.

It's important to note that when one person becomes silent and stops responding to the other, frustration and anger can be the result. If you feel overwhelmed or shutting down, you may need to take a break from the discussion. Just let her know you'll return to the conversation as soon as possible, and then remember to follow up. Follow-up is essential. Keep your promise and return to the conversation. You may even want to refer back to the "remain calm" section to recenter for the next discussion.

Likewise, if you notice your daughter is clamming up, give her some space and check back in later. This will give her time to reset.

Be Specific and Productive

Be precise about what is bothering you. Try not to generalize. Avoid words like "never" or "always." These sweeping terms are usually inaccurate anyway and will (almost) always heighten tensions. Instead of using hyperbolic language that could cause her to feel powerless, focus on what you're feeling in the moment. Vague complaints are also challenging to address, and tackling each specific item productively is important.

Demonstrate Active Listening Every Day

Practice active listening when your daughter tells you something important, and avoid interrupting them when they're speaking, even if you disagree. Active listening is the cornerstone of all effective communication. It involves not only hearing the words she says but also understanding her emotions and perspectives. Validate your daughter by maintaining eye contact and providing nonverbal cues like nodding to show that you're engaged. Your body language matters.

Be present in the conversation and take her feelings and criticisms seriously. Don't be distracted by external forces. Never multitask while she is communicating with you. Put down those dishes. Put away your phone. Don't engage in the activity if it takes your eyes or thoughts away from her. Listen to and reflect on what she is saying before responding. Be sure to ask open-ended questions to encourage her to share more, and remember one thing: if she's communicating it, it's important.

Use Neutral Language to Maintain Harmony

Your choice of words can significantly impact the tone of your communication. To prevent defensiveness and promote understanding, avoid accusatory language and instead focus on the specific behavior or issue. Accusations will lead your daughter to focus on defending herself rather than understanding you or your perspective. Instead, discuss how an action made you feel.

Use "We" Statements

Using "we" instead of "you" statements conveys that you are in this together, working as a team to resolve a problem. It's important to communicate that you are practicing empathy and acknowledging her feelings and perspectives. This is something healthy for her to see so that she can model that behavior.

For instance, if the issue concerns you being frustrated with your daughter over her portion of the household responsibilities, using "we" statements can help you address the concern without making her feel attacked or accused.

Don't Say This
"You never do your chores."

Instead, Say This
"We seem to have a lot of chores piling up, and it's becoming a bit overwhelming. Can we find a new routine so we both have time to relax?"

Emphasizing "we" makes the conversation more about finding solutions together rather than pointing fingers, which can often lead to a more productive and less confrontational discussion. It also empowers your child to feel like her input matters.

Use "I" Statements

Expressing yourself without becoming overly aggressive can be challenging when faced with a conflict, especially if your daughter is pushing your buttons or has been acting out a lot recently. To help de-escalate the situation and clarify your point, an "I" or an assertive statement is an effective psychiatrist-approved approach. Suppose there's a conflict where you feel she wants to hang out with her friends and never do anything with you and the rest of the family anymore.

Don't Say This
"You are always with your friends and never spend any time with us! You don't care about your family."

Instead, Say This
"I feel a little neglected when you spend a lot of time with your friends, and we don't get to spend as much quality time together. I value our family and would like all of us to find a balance that allows us to enjoy each other's company."

This "I" statement expresses your feelings and needs without blaming or accusing your daughter. After all, if you're having this conversation, it's because your daughter is a teenager and is becoming independent. Time with friends is a good thing! But still, being open and honest about your feelings and not pointing fingers like she has done something wrong will make it a lot more productive—and who knows, she may even toss you a bone and hang out with you in lieu of hanging with her pals.

Using language that emphasizes how you feel is much more effective communication and is less likely to result in her shutting down or getting angry. It also aids in your daughter's ability to empathize and see things from your perspective. Here's another example:

Don't Say This
"You never do the dishes." (This is also likely a generalization.)

Instead, Say This
"I feel frustrated when I come home and find the sink full of dishes—because I want to come home to a clean space. I would like it if we worked on this together."

Speaking this way avoids tactics of attack, critique, and criticism, which usually lead to more hostility and defensiveness. In general, using "I" messages can create a constructive dialogue about the true causes of any conflict by avoiding aggressive behaviors and fostering effective communication.

Appreciate Silence with CDs

For the CD daughter, silence is often a way to process their thoughts and emotions. It's essential to appreciate and understand this aspect of their communication style:

- Allow your CD daughter time to gather their thoughts before discussing important matters.

- Avoid pressuring her to speak immediately after a conflict; they may need time to reflect.

- Create a safe space where silence is not perceived as a negative response but as a part of the communication process.

Offer Regular Verbal Affirmations to MYs

MY daughters thrive on verbal affirmations and emotional expression. Here's how to make your MY daughter feel valued and loved:

- Compliment her genuinely and frequently, acknowledging her strengths and positive qualities.

- Express your love verbally with affectionate language.

- Communicate your appreciation for her efforts and ongoing support.

Understand That Your Daughter May Communicate Differently Than You

Both CDs and MYs have distinct personal boundaries. Respecting these boundaries is vital to a harmonious relationship. Therefore, it's important to have open and honest discussions about your respective boundaries and comfort zones. You shouldn't push your daughter beyond her comfort zone, whether they need personal space or social engagement—even if this level of care conflicts with your needs. Creating a balance that respects both your daughter's and your needs for personal growth and reflection is critical in communicating and growing with each other. Establishing ground rules regarding when to compromise is a great idea when setting personal boundaries with one another.

Allow Your Daughter to Express Her Feelings in a Safe Environment

All children should live in an environment where they feel emotionally safe and supported. Your daughter should feel that her feelings are heard, accepted, understood, and met with empathy. This will build a healthy home environment and strong family bonds built upon trust, safety, and empathy.

First and foremost, tune in to your daughter and listen to her. Let her express how she is feeling without jumping in to tell them how she *should* be feeling or even how to fix it. You are there for comfort, above all else.

While she's expressing herself with you, do not distract or dismiss any of her feelings. Everyone is entitled to feel what they feel, and your daughter is the best judge of how something made her feel.

Even if you do not agree with how she is reacting, or feeling, to a particular situation, it's important not to dismiss it. Let her feel what she is feeling. It is important that children learn from a young age to cope with feelings. Brushing her off will make things even more difficult to cope with later in life.

Demonstrate Healthy Communication in and outside the Home

Children are interesting creatures. About as interesting as they come, in fact. They make jokes and share weird, and often ridiculous, stories. They truly can be spontaneous and ridiculous. This shows creativity and imagination—and these things are also perfectly okay to communicate.

Never brush your child off, even when what they want to communicate seems silly. Instead of just laughing them off, consider talking with them, whether it's about their favorite character or about that weird piece of lint they found in their belly button.

Let Your Daughter Take the Lead

All forms of communication begin with starting a conversation, and it's always good practice for you to demonstrate how active listening works. Let your daughter lead the conversation, and you be on the active listening end of things.

Ask Her Thoughts and Opinions

Communicate with her by asking her opinions about some recent movie or TV show you watched or even the book you might have read at bedtime. Not only will she enjoy conversing with you, but this will also be practice for analytical skills later down the road.

Reverse the Role

Now that you have let your daughter take the lead, ask that she show you what she's learned in communication. Make it a game. Tell her to pay close attention to your story and see if she can remember certain aspects. Encourage her to ask questions too.

Embrace Emotional Expression

Throughout your daughter's development, she will be constantly receiving messages and information from the world around her. These little messages will help shape her and the way she acknowledges and understands feelings.

Often, children receive the message that the only acceptable emotion is happiness, so make sure she doesn't feel ashamed when she isn't happy. Do your best to acknowledge and accept all of her emotions—even the not-so-pleasant ones. Let her know that it's okay to feel the tough and challenging emotions—as long as she's willing to talk them out.

You can help her understand more emotions by pointing out storybook characters or TV show characters or even by sharing your own feelings with her at times. Children learn by modeling. What better way for her to learn modeling behavior than under your supervision and care?

When she is expressing an emotion, label it. Tell her what you are seeing or hearing her do that leads you to believe she is feeling that specific emotion too. This will help her not only understand herself and her own emotions but learn empathy for others experiencing the same.

Show Your Daughter That You're Human Too

One of the most important qualities of healthy relationships is authenticity. It is crucial that you be who you are, no matter how flawed you are (as long as it's appropriate and healthy). Being authentic in this way creates a sense of connection that is framed in openness and trust. You are being honest with your daughter in a relationship creates connection, openness, trust, and acceptance.

The truth is that there isn't a person in the world who doesn't get sad, angry, frustrated, or scared from time to time. Sometimes, these feelings can even have a decent grip and stay for a while; and in the middle of that, your daughter will be watching everything you do.

It's completely understandable that parents might want to protect their children from the grown-up or negative details. However, research has shown that putting up a happy front is not what is best for your children.

Parents who try to "be perfect" for their children lower that authenticity bond between them. This makes your child feel as though she can't trust you. Think about it—if she thinks you're lying about how you're feeling, why should she think you're telling the truth about other things? Also, if you don't want to talk about the way you feel, why should she talk about how she feels?

Key Takeaways

Effective communication forms the foundation of all healthy and flourishing relationships. It goes beyond the confines of personality types, but learning about them can be a great place to start.

This chapter has explored how you might engage with your daughter on a deeper level, whether she exhibits characteristics of CDs or MYs.

Start difficult discussions by expressing feelings without instigating conflicts. It is important, no matter what happens, to remain calm and collect yourself before delving headfirst into the conversation. Remember, your daughter is more likely to consider your perspective if she feels that she can voice her concerns without you jumping off the deep end or responding out of anger.

The best ways to express yourself without conflict is to:

- **Express Feelings with Words, Not Actions:** If you feel anger rising to an uncontrollable level, take a step back and return to the conversation after you've calmed down. Consider engaging in other activities that help you regain your composure. Encourage your daughter to do the same. Use methods like walking, deep breathing, or journaling to manage strong emotions constructively.

- **Address One Issue at a Time:** Avoid resorting to the "kitchen sink" approach. Focus on one issue at a time when discussing conflicts with your daughter.

- **Resist Underhandedness:** Steer clear of using underhanded or hurtful tactics when discussing sensitive topics with your daughter. Attacking her in sensitive areas only fosters distrust, anger, and vulnerability, which is counterproductive to communication.

- **Be Specific and Productive:** When expressing concerns, be specific and avoid making generalized statements using words like "never" or "always." Broad complaints are challenging to address and usually aren't even true.

Once the two of you are able to communicate effectively, make sure that you are demonstrating active listening skills during conversations and that you're using neutral language. "I" and "we" statements are best to be employed to emphasize that you are working together for a common goal and not that you are attacking her.

CDs may be a little less vocal during communications, and that's okay. Appreciate the silence. Allow her the space and time to collect her thoughts and feelings. Avoid pressuring her to speak immediately after a conflict, and create a safe environment where silence is just considered a part of the communication process.

MYs, on the other hand, don't do as well with silence. Make sure that you are offering verbal affirmations to help her feel safe and loved during communication. Compliment her genuinely.

Finally, understanding that your daughter may communicate differently than you is just as important as communicating at all. Recognize and respect her unique boundaries and comfort zones. Allow her time and space to communicate and express her feelings—in her way, even if you don't agree with them. Remember, no one knows how she is feeling more than her. Listen actively and avoid dismissing those feelings. And above all else, show her that you're human too. Be authentic in your heart-to-hearts and, although it is essential to protect your child from the real world, let her see that you also experience challenging emotions. Demonstrating that you can handle these feelings empowers her to understand that she can do the same.

Remember, it's not about speaking the loudest but resonating the deepest. Effective communication is the only way to proper understanding, empathy, and establishing a robust, flourishing relationship. By applying these strategies, you can cultivate a more profound connection with your girl. As they say, it takes two to tango, and being conscious of your daughter's steps is paramount!

Chapter Three

Emotional Closeness

In Chapter 3, we delve into nurturing a strong parent-child relationship.

At the end of the day, your daughter relies on you to provide her with the care and knowledge it takes to develop into a mature adult in the future. So, in essence, your daughter's development hinges on the quality of the emotional bond you share with her. For both CD and MY daughters, communication truly is key, and it opens up the door to strong emotional bonds and closeness.

Understanding the distinct emotional needs of your daughter, no matter her personality type, is vital. In this chapter, we will explore the art of talking to your daughter, engaging in meaningful interactions, and fostering an environment of open, judgment-free communication. Use this chapter as a guide to teach you how to take the lead in developing a deeper bond by merely showing respect for her mind and unique expression. Reinforce your love for her through meaningful gestures and praise, no matter if she is a CD or an MY. These strategies can help you be more emotionally connected with her for the rest of your life.

Talk to Your Daughter

No matter the age of your daughter, it is critical to talk to her; just as Chapter 2 suggests, communication is one of the major key players in having and maintaining a healthy relationship.

As parents, the primary concern is keeping your children safe and cared for—but what happens after they're grown?

You want your kids to love you enough to come back home occasionally. To do this, you must foster healthy relationships from the beginning.

Talking is the first step.

From just outside the womb, an infant cries. This is a human being's first line of communication. Whether it's a cry that says, "I need a change" or "I'm hungry" or "I don't feel good" or "I'm just fussy"—they're all lines of communication. As parents, you start to recognize the difference between these cries too.

Starting when children are young, even from infancy, the way you interact with them helps shape how they respond to you and to other people in their lives. It is critical to understand the importance of having caring conversations with your daughter to aid her in growing into a compassionate and resilient person.

By paying attention to her cues and how she responds, you will be able to show her that she is loved for who she is and also show her how to trust people and offer her skills to manage all these great, big emotions she has felt—or will feel as she gets older.

Age plays a factor in how you talk and communicate with your daughter, but no matter the age, it's important that you approach her with compassion and understanding. This will teach her how to approach others with compassion and understanding.

Speaking to your daughter will change over time, as she gets older, but certain conversations you should always have with her.

Tell Her That Expressing Herself Is Important

It is often preferable that your daughter be in a good mood, no matter her age: from being fussy as a baby to toddler meltdowns and tantrums, to moody and grumbly preteens and teens. However, it is important to note that your daughter having unpleasant feelings such as sadness, disappointment, frustration, anger, and fear is completely normal, and it's healthy for her to express those feelings with you.

These feelings are often expressed through crying, temper tantrums, and challenging behaviors—which can all leave you feeling completely frustrated.

However, your feelings serve a purpose—and so do hers. They tell her—and you—what she needs. By paying attention to her feelings and the way she expresses them, you show her that how she feels matters to you and that she can always count on you to do your best to address her needs.

When your daughter's feelings challenge you, ask yourself these questions:

- Are the expectations I have for her reasonable and realistic?
- Am I holding her to a higher standard than I hold myself?
- Have I taught her what to do when she feels this way?

Let Her Know There Are Multiple Ways to Express Feelings

Telling your daughter that it's okay to feel frustrated but not okay to scream at you is a great example of healthy parenting.

While it is helpful for an infant to cry and scream when they are hurt or upset, as children get older, they should have more tools in their tool belts to not have to express themselves this way anymore. As your daughter's brain matures and her vocabulary grows, encourage her to communicate with her words rather than tantrums or cries.

The best way to do this is to talk with her about your family's rules—your emotion rules. This is a tool that has helped so many families find what works for them. The way you create these rules is by asking yourself the question: How do I want my children and the adults in my family to show emotions?

By utilizing this tool, you can set expectations early, and when a child goes against the emotion rules that you set forth, you can discuss it with them openly.

A fun way to describe emotions or expressions is by using storybooks or fun emotional charts to help your child see that everyone has feelings and to help her understand how to recognize those feelings. Reading together offers a chance to discuss the challenging feelings that characters may feel and what they do to overcome obstacles.

Teaching children how to not only understand emotions but express them takes time, practice, role modeling, and lots of repetition. But it is essential that you teach your daughter that there are a million different ways to express what it is that she's feeling.

Explain That Everyone Must Learn and Making Mistakes Is Normal

Through your interactions and conversations, you impact *how* your daughters learn as well as *what* they learn. It is important for your daughter to understand that everyone has to learn and that making mistakes and learning for them is all part of the process.

When children struggle to do something, this can feel frustrating, especially when you feel you have explained the situation or process with which they are struggling.

This can potentially be harmful when expressed outwardly. It could lead your daughter to giving up or her self-esteem lowering. Instead, help her turn challenging moments into learning opportunities.

Highlight her efforts and encourage her by saying that making mistakes is all part of the learning process. It takes time, problem-solving, and above all—patience. Explain that it's important that she never gives up.

Taking these few steps may be a challenge at first, especially in the moment, but it's critical that you practice this. Children with the mindset that every struggle is an opportunity to learn and persevere tend to outperform children who believe that all of their abilities come naturally. The mentality of "You either have it, or you don't" isn't true, and it's crucial that you don't instill that ideology in your daughter.

Reaffirm That You Are Being the Best Parent You Can Be

Always, always, always show your daughter what you want her to learn by doing it yourself. As parents, you need to lead by example. For example, if you feel overwhelmed in a situation and you don't feel you have the answer, talk to her about it. Tell her that although you're trying your best to listen and figure out what she needs, you aren't sure what the right answer is just yet.

Take this sort of modeling a step further, and if you overreact to a situation, apologize. Let your daughter know that you're sorry that you lost your temper and yelled at her when you shouldn't have.

Imagine if your teenage daughter came to you one morning and said, "I was thinking about how I acted last night, and I shouldn't have yelled at you that way. I'm very sorry." Showing her proper communication and showing her that you're being your best every day will encourage her to mimic you and do the same. Above all else, this sort of behavior will show her day in and day out that you are being the best parent you can be.

Show Your CD You Respect Her Mind

Regularly engage with your CD daughter and listen to her thoughts and the way she expresses them. Encourage regular check-ins and be consistent about following up. Listen to her, be engaged, and above all—let her speak.

It is important for CDs to feel respected for their minds. A great consideration would be to make a fun debate out of things she would like to see change in the household. Or offer her the chance to write it out if the game feels too overwhelming. Regardless of how you do it, make sure you show her that you are invested in her, appreciate her thoughts, and acknowledge them. However, before she is able to speak her mind, you must first teach her how to properly develop it.

Developing Language and Communication

From a very young age, children are fascinated by dramatic characters, interesting plots, and unfamiliar places. These things spark their imagination and their curiosity. The very moment your daughter hears the words "Once upon a time," it's game-on for her mind. Her attention becomes fully immersed in the story and imagination is invoked.

Telling your daughter stories helps her enrich her vocabulary. Of course, speaking to your daughter in general helps her develop language, but using language in context to a story introduces a whole other narrative. The meaning of the words becomes richer—and a lot more interesting. For toddlers, who are new to the world, every story can be chockfull of information. For example, telling a story about a rabbit eating a carrot teaches your little one that rabbits eat carrots, which can then help her understand that different animals have different diets.

Telling Stories Supports Cognitive and Emotional Development

Many studies have shown that telling stories has great benefits. They not only support cognitive development, but they elevate children's linguistic abilities—as well as increase their reasoning skills. Children who read more books, overall, have been proven to develop better emotional skills and have an increased ability to be attentive and empathetic. The American Academy of Pediatrics recommends that parents should start telling stories to their children as early as possible—even infancy.

Not only is this a great opportunity to aid your children in academic pursuits and emotional development, but it is also a wonderful opportunity to bond with your daughter. It is a moment of quality one-on-one time that involves joint interest, no distraction, and above all else—fun.

Reading a story to your daughter can be beneficial in so many ways to enrich her mind. If you want to set yourself up for success, ensure that:

- **The Timing Is Right:** Choose a time when you and your daughter are both relaxed but not too tired to read and enjoy the story. This will encourage your little one's ability to listen for longer. If bedtime is the best time to read, try to start your routine a half hour early, so you both are awake enough to finish!

- **You Choose the Right Story or Book:** Telling a story is meaningful when it fits a child's age and developmental stage. Make sure the story you are reading is age-appropriate and is made to keep your daughter entertained. For one to two-year-olds, choose a baby book with simple sentences and lots of illustrations. It should involve familiar elements from daily life, like going to sleep, brushing teeth, or saying good-bye. Steer away from complex stories or lengthy ones. As your daughter ages, the books should become lengthier and hold more depth.

- **You Are an Active Storyteller:** Bring the story to life by reading dynamically. Using voices, asking questions, and relating what you're reading to your child's own experiences really sets your reading experience up for success. Be expressive and keep your daughter captivated by really getting into the role. Bring energy, be theatrical, and sell it!

She is more likely to pay attention, and research has shown that active and expressive storytelling that really engages a child improves memory and academic success.

- **You Listen:** Pay attention to your daughter's reactions and questions. Make sure that you respond to her curiosity.

Moments like this start your daughter up for success right away. It shows that not only do you respect her mind, but you also are invested in it. Once you help her develop into an independent thinker, continue respecting her perspectives. Show her that you appreciate and love her mind—no matter what stage of life she is in.

Show Your MY You Respect Her Expression

Your MY is likely a social butterfly and might even be one of the boldest people you have ever met. Respect her expression of herself and of her emotions.

This could be in bold clothing, arts, theatrics, or even screaming from the rooftops. Whatever the case, make sure you show your MY little girl that you respect her need for bold expression and more than anything, make sure you reaffirm that not only do you respect it, but you enjoy it.

In fact, a blessing to some parents—and possibly a curse—what you see with your MY is typically what you get. Your MY daughter is likely upfront about her emotions—when she can properly identify them, that is. If she doesn't yet have the necessary language skills to identify the feelings she's experiencing, she will do so in other ways.

MYs will readily express laughter, excitement, tears, frustration, and anger through their voices and body language. Everything is external for your MY daughter. This can be frustrating when the emotions aren't positive ones, but it is still important that you respect the expression anyway. She is doing what she can to be open with you about what she is feeling. It is more important that you show her how to healthily regulate rather than dismiss her or be bothered by outbursts.

Just as a CD daughter needs quiet time for expressing her feelings, an MY daughter needs to be verbal or physical.

Ways to appropriately show that you respect your MY daughter's expression are:

- By accepting her feelings.
- By telling her that whatever she feels is okay.
- By teaching her ways to express her emotions healthily.

Have Meaningful Interactions and Outings with Your Daughter

A great way to create emotional closeness with your daughter is by doing one-on-one outings with her or having one-on-one interactions. This can also be something you and your co-parent do with your daughter together. If you have more than one child, try to divide one-on-one (or both parents to one child) attention evenly. It is important that your daughter feels like an individual rather than just being grouped in with her siblings or other family members.

There are several ways to have meaningful interactions and outings with your daughter. Make sure you take her personality type into consideration as well as her personal interests and hobbies.

Don't be afraid to try something new; maybe do something outside the box.

Create a Family Tree: Make it fun! Making a family tree will not only give your daughter one-on-one time with you to grow an emotional closeness. It will also give her an opportunity to learn about other members of her family. Tell stories of good memories you have with each branch of the family tree. Go as far down the tree as you can. Share lessons learned, experiences had. Invite your daughter to shape her own branch and discuss where she wants her branch to go.

Movie with a Twist: You all watch movies, and while movies can be an effective tool in spending bonding time with your children (especially teenagers who don't always want to express themselves with words), it can also be overused. Consider doing a movie night—but with a twist.

Find a good book that spawned a good movie, and then read it together as a family over the course of a week. The movie and popcorn should make a fun finale and kick off some interesting discussion afterward. This turns a two-hour movie into a weeklong process of bonding and invokes wonderful discussion pieces instead of just sitting in silence.

Plan a Family Event: This could be a big vacation or a small event or get-together. Letting her have a say in the planning process teaches her how to effectively plan an event, but it also gives her a sense of responsibility and accountability. Above all else—it shows that you trust your daughter.

Plan an Imaginary Road Trip: Here's how this works. Define the limits (time, cost, reality vs. fantasy, etc.), set them up around the table and brainstorm (all ideas are acceptable), then write out the plan. Because it's not actually happening, it's a safe way to get inside everyone's dreams and find out their likes and dislikes (this is especially great if you have more than one child). Who knows, you may end up taking the trip one day—and even if you don't, it's a wonderful exercise to get to know your children better.

Regardless of the activity or conversation, having meaningful interactions with your daughter is as simple as listening and being present. Being present means taking a moment to clear your mind of all distractions so that your focus is only on connecting with her. Remember that being with her is the priority, as is helping to support her growth and development.

When you are faced with tasks throughout the day, it can be easy to get distracted. With mounting paperwork or household responsibilities, there is plenty out there to take hold of your attention. Reminding yourself that being present with her, though, is first and foremost your most important role will help you prioritize the other tasks.

Engage in Activities Your CD or MY Enjoy

Your daughter, no matter her personality type, will crave attention from you. By engaging in activities that she enjoys, you will open up a whole new world of closeness between the two of you.

Your CD daughter may like a quiet evening at home or even at a movie theater. And if your daughter is an MY, she may prefer to go to an arcade or to a skating rink with some of her friends in tow. Do things you know will make her happy, and enjoy doing them yourself.

Consider trying something new together to help her discover a whole new world of interests too. This will create a deeper bond between the two of you, and you never know, you both might discover that you share your new favorite thing.

For CD daughters, consider:

- Starting a book club between the two of you.
- Going skating.
- Playing games or doing a puzzle together.
- Gardening together.
- Staring a collection.
- Learning how to knit together.

Alternatively, for your MY daughter, consider:

- Trying your hand at tie-dying.
- Learning a new language together.
- Cooking together.
- Going camping or biking.
- Rock-climbing.
- Volunteering together.

Create an Environment That Allows for Open, Judgment-Free Communication

To be nonjudgmental in the parenting sense means several things, and you are often given several opportunities to test this out on any given day.

Assume the Best of Your Daughter

Being nonjudgmental, first and foremost, means looking at your child in the present moment and assuming the best of her.

For example, if your daughter gets home after school and is grouchy and complaining about everything, you might want to say that she's just being a brat. And of course, you will want her to learn how to behave herself. So, in your best attempt to discipline her, you start piling consequences on her, hoping it "teaches" her something.

But here are some questions to consider before you do that:

- Will it actually work?
- Can you follow through on all of these consequences?
- Does it help your relationship with your daughter?

Instead, the more appropriate action may be to think to yourself: Why is she behaving this way? Did she have a bad day? Did she get a terrible night's rest?

Consider these options.

It could just be that she is tired and hungry. So, instead of coming down on her, consider offering her a snack and ask her to relax for a bit. After she is well-regulated, then you can have a chat together about how she was feeling and how she might behave differently in the future. This is a great time to discuss your emotion rules too.

Avoid Classifications

Being nonjudgmental also means other things, such as not classifying days as good or bad or their behavior as good or bad. Would you want someone to judge you or your parenting as good or bad based on one particular day or another? By reading this book, it's clear that you are doing your best. And the cold hard truth is sometimes your best fluctuates from day to day—and that's okay!

Classifying or generalizing your daughter puts her inside a box that she may not belong in and not only does that disappoint you, but it also could cause harmful self-imagery for her.

Keep the Past in the Past

Practice not dredging up the past. Even if it just happened this morning. If you carry the fact that your daughter yelled at you this morning into this afternoon's dysregulated behavior, it could very well only exacerbate the situation by making her feel even more negative.

It is entirely possible that your daughter may be actually feeling guilty and defensive about her morning behavior, and if you join in on that, blaming or shaming behavior will only solidify her perspective.

You can rehabilitate the morning situation with your daughter by saying something like, "I wonder if you might be feeling upset over yelling at me this morning and wondering if I'm still mad at you." If she agrees, a reply could be, "It did hurt my feelings, but it actually made me worry about what might happen if you yelled at one of your teachers or your friends like that. What do you think?"

If your daughter doesn't agree that is how she is feeling, it would still be good to acknowledge that you are not holding a grudge from this morning.

As parents, when children find a way to push away from you, it is your job to set aside your own feelings. At the end of the day, you are adults, with developed cognitive skills. You are the ones in charge of finding a path to reconnection. If you struggle with this, please seek the advice of professionals. It is important to see your daughter how she is in the current moment, without holding her past (no matter how recent) against her.

It is entirely possible that she will have a "rap sheet" that is pages long. However, it is important to wipe the slate clean often and see your daughter as you did the day you first met her, even if she is an annoying teenager.

Let Your CD or MY Tell You What They Need and When They Need It

Studies show that there are seven emotional needs that your daughter has. These are universal, no matter the personality type she possesses. However, some children may differ in the amount of each that they receive and are shown. These seven needs are discussed throughout this book and are a common theme in all human emotional needs.

Get to know your daughter through open communication and let her tell you or show you what she needs from you and when. Encourage her to talk to you about emotional shortcomings in your relationship, even from a young age, because meeting her needs is critical to your emotional closeness.

Besides, when kids' needs are met, parenting is a lot easier. You will discover if their needs are being met, you will be met with far fewer power struggles and arguments. You will discover that your communication will improve, and you will discover a much deeper connection to your daughter.

The seven needs are:

- **Unconditional Love:** It shouldn't come as a surprise to know that your daughter needs unconditional love. Of course, this feels easy because as parents, you love your children.

But it's important to really consider the meaning of the word "unconditional." If you truly express love to your kids unconditionally, then your love and affection cannot be bound by anything your child does, says, or feels. This can be difficult, but it is important even during your arguments that you reassure your daughter that you love her endlessly.

- **Empathy:** One of the most fundamental ways to create a connection with your daughter is through being empathetic. Letting her know that you understand and sympathize with what she is going through fills her with a sense of security—which in turn lets her feel safe expressing herself with you.

- **Validation:** Of course, everyone wants to feel validated—but your daughter wants to feel validated especially. In a world that treats children—at times—as less than human, it's easy for kids to feel isolated or that their feelings aren't as important as adults' feelings. Acknowledge her feelings when she shares them with you—even just a few words will do wonders. Tell her, "That must have been really frustrating," when she's telling you a story and it's clear that she's frustrated. This gives her a sense of security, much like empathy does.

- **Boundaries:** All children—and adults—need boundaries. While providing your child with boundaries isn't an emotional need in and of itself, kids yearn for boundaries to feel emotionally stable.

- **Acceptance:** Everyone wants to feel accepted for who they are. Imagine how powerful it is for your daughter to feel completely accepted by the most important people in her life—her parents.

- **Feeling Heard:** Children, like anyone, have an emotional need to feel heard or listened to. When children don't feel heard, they act out—whether that be by yelling, screaming, throwing, or hitting. They will act out. Feeling heard supports positive self-esteem and also makes your daughter feel more open to hearing others out too.

- **Belonging:** Every human needs to feel that they belong—most importantly, belong within their family. A sense of belonging has been shown to have an effect on a person's overall well-being, cognitive performance, academic achievements, and physical health.

When all seven of these are given to your daughter, she feels what everyone on this planet yearns to feel—and that is that she is significant. Significance entails everything above. The emotional need for significance is nearly synonymous with a sense of belonging. But to feel significant, one has to feel not only that they belong but that their thoughts, opinions, and beliefs matter. Children who have their emotional needs met typically feel validated enough that they feel significant.

Praise Her

Praise your daughter—don't only point out her shortcomings or mistakes. Point out the things she does right.

Praise will nurture your daughter's sense of self. By using praise, you're showing her how to think and talk positively about themselves—and others. You're helping her learn how to recognize when she does well and feel proud of herself.

You can praise children of different ages for different things. You might praise your younger daughter for sharing her toys or for leaving the park when you ask the first time. You can praise your teenage daughter for coming home at her curfew or for starting homework without being reminded.

Studies show that children are more likely to repeat behavior that earns praise or encouragement. This means you can use praise and encouragement to change challenging behaviors.

If your daughter behaves in challenging ways, the first step is to identify the positive behavior that you want to encourage. For example, if your daughter is taking toys from other children, you might want to encourage her to take turns with toys instead. Then, watch for and praise when she does this. When you see her sharing, immediately get her attention and tell her that you liked how she shared her toys. It is crucial that you do this every time you see the positive behavior until you recognize that it is a common occurrence. Then, you can praise or encourage that specific thing less, which will give you a chance to praise her for other positive behaviors.

Try to praise your daughter much more frequently than you correct her. This will show her that she does more good than bad, give her positive self-esteem, and be more likely to make her want to correct the behaviors that are less favorable. When you feel good about your daughter's behavior, tell her.

Look for nonverbal ways to praise or encourage your child. A thumbs up, a smile, or even just a high five can all be effective ways to show your daughter that you're impressed with her efforts.

Try to make your praise appropriate to the behavior. Be sincere and enthusiastic but not over the top. She needs to see it's genuine and also develop realistic expectations for praise. It wouldn't really be appropriate to jump up and down clapping and screaming if she just said, "Thank you," when someone shared a toy. This could make her see your praise as ingenuine or have unrealistic expectations for future praise—which could also leak into adulthood.

Try to mix up rewards and also use them age-appropriately. Rewards work great for praise, when it makes sense, but they work best when they are varied, rather than repetitive. If your daughter gets the same reward every time she does something good, she may come to think of it as a normal everyday occurrence rather than a reward at all. This could also lead to her feeling unrewarded. Use praise and rewards in age-appropriate ways. For example, teenagers might not want to be praised publicly for their efforts, as it may embarrass them, whereas toddlers might love being singled out for praise in front of others.

Keep in mind that rewards can make praise and encouragement work better. But they can be overused. If you feel like you are having to use rewards or incentives often, then it is possible that the behavior is too difficult for your child to master right now.

Tell Your Daughter You Love Her

Letting your daughter know that she is loved for who she is *now* and who she *will become* builds a trusting relationship. This is commonly referred to as a positive attachment.

Build your relationship up by spending time with her, doing things she chooses to do, and paying attention to her likes and interests. During these moments, it's critical you put away distractions. Never try to multitask during quality time with your daughter.

And of course, as with all children, she will test your boundaries. During these moments, reassure her that you *love her* but *dislike her behavior*—at the moment.

Children who have that positive attachment that trust and affirmation bring typically have a laundry list of positive characteristics such as:

- Higher self-esteem.
- Better self-control.
- Stronger critical thinking.
- Better academic achievements.

- Stronger social skills.

- Greater empathy and compassion.

So, when engaging with your daughter, tell her you love her—often.

Key Takeaways

In this chapter, we explored the essence of emotional closeness with your daughter. Remember, the key to fostering a healthy parent-daughter relationship is effective communication. Talk to your daughter. No matter her age, communication is paramount. From the moment she's born, she communicates through cries and coos, and as parents, you begin to discern the meaning behind these expressions.

The way you interact with your daughter shapes her responses to you and others. Engaging in caring conversations helps her grow into a compassionate and resilient future adult. For her to do this, it's important that she understands that learning to express herself genuinely is the first step.

- **Understand That Her Emotions Are Her Way of Expressing Needs:** Her mood will vary throughout her life. From being a fussy baby to a moody preteen and teen, she'll experience various emotions, and some of them won't be the most appetizing. Acknowledge that it's normal for her to feel sadness, disappointment, or frustration, and encourage her to express these feelings because ultimately you need to understand her needs, and you can't if you don't understand her emotions.

- **Evaluate Whether Your Expectations Are Reasonable:** Make sure that you're not holding her to a higher standard than you hold yourself. It's perfectly fine for your daughter to express herself in a less-than-ideal manner at times. Talk with her, explain shortcomings if she's expressing in a way that can be harmful, and then move on. Understand that it's likely you also have your own shortcomings when expressing yourself, especially if your emotions are heightened.

- **Teach Her How to Manage Her Emotions Constructively:** Tell her that there are multiple ways of expressing oneself. While infants may cry and scream, older children should develop healthier ways to communicate. Encourage her to express herself with words and discuss your family's emotion rules.

Your interactions and conversations shape your daughter's learning. Emphasize that making mistakes and learning from them are natural parts of growth. Lead by example to show your daughter how to handle uncertainty and challenges, especially your mistakes:

- If you lose your temper, apologize and demonstrate the importance of open communication.

- Display humility and the ability to learn.

- Encourage self-reflection and improvement.

Always engage with your daughter, listen to her thoughts, and consistently follow up. Encourage her to share her ideas, thoughts, and concerns. If she is a CD, you may consider:

- Fostering respect for her intellect.

- Creating opportunities for open dialogue.

- Making her feel valued and appreciated by giving her space to collect herself and feel.

Respect your daughter's unique expression, whether it's bold clothing, arts, or theatrics. Reaffirm your appreciation for her individuality. And strengthen your emotional bond by spending quality one-on-one time with her or planning family events. Create a deeper connection through activities tailored to her interests.

- For CD daughters, consider activities like gardening or starting a book club.

- For MY daughters, try tie-dyeing, cooking, or rock-climbing.

Explore new activities together to foster a deeper bond. And also, make sure that when communicating with your daughter to invoke emotional closeness, you:

- Create an environment that allows for open and judgment-free communication.

- Let your daughter know that:
  - She is loved—unconditionally.
  - She is heard.
  - She is accepted.
  - Her feelings are validated.
  - You have set boundaries to help her feel safe.
  - You empathize with what she is feeling.
  - She belongs.

Chapter Four

Proper Socialization

In this chapter, we embark on an interesting journey that many often forget to focus on in most relationships: your social lives.

Studies show that children need proper socialization too. Human beings are social creatures. You just have to find a balance that everyone is comfortable with. In this chapter, we focus on the importance of balancing your and your daughter's social lives and how understanding the personalities of CDs and MYs aids in this attempt. This chapter focuses on how the two personality types thrive under different levels of social involvement and how it may affect your family if your daughter differs from one or both parents or even their siblings.

Understand CDs' Need for Solitude and MYs' Social Inclinations

Understanding and accommodating the distinct social needs of CDs and MYs is crucial to the overall mental well-being of everyone. While CDs tend to seek solitude and personal space for introspection and recharging, MYs often thrive in social settings, relishing vibrant interactions.

The foundation of any successful relationship is open and honest communication, of course, and once your child is able to have an opinion on the matter, it may be worth having a conversation with her about her social needs. CDs might express their need for occasional solitude and MYs their desire for social engagements. Sharing these feelings with one another fosters understanding and allows for compromises to happen.

It is entirely possible that you want to be social while your daughter doesn't. Or vice versa. It could also be possible that multiple children may also have differing ideologies about what they want socially. If you find yourself in a family with differing social needs or desires, it's important to discuss it as a family and find common ground so that everyone is comfortable.

Encourage Activities Catering to Both Personalities

Compromises aren't always possible, but they *generally* are. Understanding that some activities may be more fun for certain personality types is crucial. It is important that you encourage activities that cater to both personalities. This is even true for families who comprise all MYs or all CDs. A little variation is important in developing growth.

Negotiate Personal Space

First things first, before you engage in any activities with your daughter, establish some boundaries and negotiate how much personal space is needed. Keep in mind that CDs require alone time to rejuvenate. Encourage your CD daughter to communicate when she needs solitude and respect her space during these moments. If you—or other family members—are MYs, this time can be used for more social interactions without your CD daughter. This would allow everyone time to get what they want.

Create a Relaxing Home Environment

Designate a tranquil space within your home where CDs can retreat when they need solitude. Make it comfortable and conducive to relaxation, ensuring it serves as a great recharging space or sanctuary for them.

Balance Your Social Calendar

If you're an MY and your daughter is a CD, conduct your social activities to strike a balance between her solitude time and your socializing. Or even vice versa. Consider having specific days or times for social engagements together and then times for personal reflection. This way, both of you can feel validated.

Support Her Choices

No matter where either you or your daughter fall in the personality spectrum, support her, regardless if you are particularly happy with the choice she has made or not. For example, if she is a CD and expresses a desire for solitude while you want to go out with the rest of the family, it is recommended that you respect her wishes. Remember, if she communicates her needs, they're likely important to her. You can address a need for her to engage in a social event with you at another time if she truly needs solitude.

Set Realistic Expectations

Recognize that striking a balance between going out and staying in (if you differ in personality types) might require a lot of communication and compromise. CDs may need to step out of their comfort zone occasionally, while MYs may need to accept that solitude is essential for CDs.

Plan Activities That Meet Your CD's or MY's Social Needs

Planning activities that cater to your daughter's social needs can be a delightful way to not only ensure her needs are met but also to strengthen your bond with her. CDs and MYs have distinct preferences, and finding a middle ground can be difficult if your personality differs from hers, but once you do find it, your connection can grow stronger.

Discuss Interests

It is important to initiate conversations about her hobbies and interests together while remembering that CDs often enjoy solitary or small-group activities like reading, hiking, or crafting, while MYs might be inclined toward social outings like meeting with friends, attending parties, or participating in group sports. Understanding her interests is the first step in planning activities to participate in together.

Compile a Shared List

Create a list of activities that interest both of you (or all of your children, if you have multiple kids). These could include weekend hikes in nature, cooking classes, movie nights, volunteering, or even trying a new hobby together. Focus on activities that everyone enjoys first—and then make plans to do those things!

Schedule Regular "Me Time" for Everyone

Acknowledging the fact that all of you may need your own personal "me" time is essential to keeping a peaceful home. It's possible that CDs may need occasional alone time for introspection, and MYs in the family may crave social interaction that other family members may not want to engage in at the moment. Plan your schedules to include designated "me time" so that each of you can pursue your individual interests.

Rotate Activity Choices

Alternate between activities that align with CDs' and MYs' preferences. For instance, if you enjoyed a social event one weekend, plan a quieter, more introspective activity for the next.

Experiment with New Experiences

Keep the family dynamics fresh and exciting by occasionally stepping out of comfort zones and encouraging everyone else to do the same. Trying new things together can be an adventure that strengthens the bond you all have. Whether it's taking a dance class, exploring a new hiking trail, or attending an art exhibit, your daughter will definitely appreciate your efforts in breaking up the monotony.

Balance Frequency

Ensure a balance between activities that cater to each personality. Avoid overwhelming your CD daughter with frequent social events or leaving your MY daughter feeling isolated. Open communication is key to finding balance. Make sure you follow Chapter 2 recommendations on how to open a dialogue if anyone feels like there is an imbalance.

Reflect and Adjust as Needed

Periodically review how everyone in the family feels about these social activities, and communicate with one another. Have your own thoughts about the balance of your activities and whether you feel represented in your outings, and ask your partner and your children to do the same. Be willing to adjust your approach based on their feedback. After all, participating in activities that everyone enjoys—even if you all differ in personality types—can really foster an understanding within the family and strengthen your family unit. At the end of the day, you all want to feel heard and understood by the people you love. By valuing your daughter's (and other children's) personalities and trying to accommodate preferences, you'll strengthen your connection and create lasting memories together in the process.

Life is all about adventures. Trying new things and embracing the fact that you are all unique individuals with your own interests will make your lives together go a lot more smoothly. It can even make it that much more exciting and adventurous. Just make sure you celebrate your daughter's passions and encourage her in all of your endeavors together.

Appreciate MYs' Need for Social Outings

We have spoken about MYs and their social endeavors, but by supporting your daughter in what she is drawn to, such as her social endeavors, you are strengthening the emotional bond between you. Ways to support and encourage those endeavors include:

- Encouraging her attendance at parties and celebrating her for the social butterfly she is.

- Actively participating in social events and outings with her.

- Respecting her independence and the time she sets aside for friends.

- Planning surprise parties for her.

MYs thrive on social interactions and exciting experiences. If your daughter is an MY, it's essential that you understand and even respect her need for lively social engagements, even if it isn't your thing. MYs' enthusiasm is infectious, so hopefully that won't be an issue, but it's important to help her feel validated in her need for social activities. So, make sure you embrace her zest for life and be open to trying new things. Your willingness to participate in her adventures and show an interest in her interests can truly boost the parent-child bond.

Recognize Her Energy and Support Her Social Initiatives

MYs often bring a lot of energy to social situations. Even if it isn't your thing, acknowledge and celebrate this quality your daughter brings to the table. Understand that her being enthusiastic about socializing is part of who she is. Encourage her to pursue social activities she might be passionate about. This could be joining clubs, attending parties or events, or going out with her friends. No matter what it is, make sure that you're supportive.

MYs enjoy excitement and new experiences. If you want to support her, you can show your interest in making her happy by planning outings or adventures that align with her interests. This could be hiking an adventurous trail with you and a pack of her closest friends, taking her to a parent-daughter dance, or exploring new places. In any case, share her enthusiasm for that fun and adventure.

Remember, MYs appreciate spontaneity, so surprise her with unplanned outings or last-minute activities or plans. These surprises can inject excitement into her and make her feel valued.

Set Age-Appropriate Boundaries for Your Daughter

Many parents are reluctant to set limits because they don't want to upset their children or incite power struggles. However, not establishing clear boundaries is proven to create various issues for your child. Kids need limits to learn self-regulation. Without rules, they have no idea how to cope because they have never had to cope. This, in turn, leads to issues in their adulthood.

As parents, you need to adjust the way you interpret boundaries. Instead of viewing limits as negative, reframe them as opportunities for growth. When you give your child rules to follow, you allow them to practice managing emotions, solving problems, and cooperating with others. These characteristics are crucial to forming healthy relationships in the future.

Giving your daughter clear boundaries helps her build her emotional and cognitive skills. Benefits of this are:

- **Improved Confidence:** When children have guidelines, they understand what is expected of them and in turn are able to feel competent and valuable when they follow them.

- **Reduced Anxiety:** Rules and routines make your child's environment feel more secure and predictable.

- **Stronger Values:** Reinforcing good behavior through rules teaches your daughter that her actions impact everyone around her. This can strengthen the family unit and teach values such as empathy and consideration.

- **Better Boundaries:** Children raised in overly permissive households often have difficulty setting limits with others, which can make them vulnerable to bullying and abuse. By setting limits with your daughter, you are setting the bar. You are teaching that it is not only okay to have boundaries in place but also that it's normal and healthy.

How to Set Age-Appropriate Limits for Your Daughter

There is, of course, a right way and a wrong way to set limits and boundaries for your child. For rules to be effective, they must be enforceable, consistent, easy to understand, and above all age-appropriate.

It's a balancing act to find what is most appropriate for your child, specifically. Having too high expectations for your child can set her up for failure. On the other hand, holding her back with overly restrictive limits can hinder her autonomy and confidence.

Before you start establishing rules, clarify what values and behaviors you want to instill in your daughter. For example, are honesty, politeness, and compassion your top priorities? If so, it makes sense to establish that there will be no lying, harming others, or any sort of rudeness. Ensure that you model and uphold these values yourself. Your children mimic your behaviors.

Infants (Birth to One Year Old): Though infants are too young to understand rules, they still need to have structure. To help your baby feel secure, put them on a schedule and be consistent.

Toddlers (One to Three Years Old): This is a difficult age. Being realistic and flexible is essential when parenting a toddler. Kids in this age bracket need to explore, and when you add in poor impulse control—it gets a little hectic.

It is essential to give your toddler space to have this curiosity and explore but also keep her safe. Get potentially dangerous obstacles out of the area so she can play freely. Then, focus on teaching her how to share without displays of aggression, such as hitting or biting, when she doesn't want to.

When you need to correct your toddler, the best approach is to say something simple, such as "No hitting." Short, sweet, and to the point is the best method. Children this age cannot understand lectures. Redirection is key here. Get her attention on something more positive, and if that doesn't work, remove her from the situation that has now become triggering.

School-Age Children (Six to Eleven Years Old): For kids this age, as a parent, it is critical to reduce uncertainty and stress. Your school-age child needs to have a set list of rules and responsibilities at home. She should know what is expected of her each and every day—and at all points during the day. Kids this age benefit from calendars and schedules posted where they can view them.

Adolescents (Thirteen to Eighteen Years Old): During your daughter's adolescent years, you should gradually cease overseeing her daily schedule and instead let her make choices when she does her tasks. Taking a step back in this manner is necessary to allow her to grow and learn how to manage her time and life independently.

It can be difficult when you know your daughter isn't making a good decision, but allowing her to learn this on her own is a great benefit. If she has had structure her entire life to this point, there is a good chance she will stick with the routine anyway.

At this age, it is most important to have and maintain rules that enforce strong moral values and positive conduct. Remember that your teenager has her own thoughts and opinions and respect is a two-way street.

Even when you feel like your daughter is being distant or challenging you, do not belittle her. You should also require her to uphold a certain standard of behavior when she doesn't agree with your decisions.

If you feel like your relationship with your teen daughter is becoming strained, get her input. Collaborating may be helpful. Your teenage daughter will often be more willing to cooperate when she believes she has had input and the rules are fair to her. This helps her feel heard and understood. Using this strategy prevents arguments and also gives her a dose of what it's like to set her own rules and boundaries in a household.

When to Get Help Setting Limits

As kids get older, discipline tends to become increasingly more challenging. It is not uncommon for children to have communication issues and for a disconnect to appear during adolescence.

If you ever feel like you've "lost control" of your daughter, don't give up. Instead, seek out a trained professional, such as a licensed family therapist. They can often help bridge a gap between a parent and child by being a third party and seeing both sides.

She needs you, no matter how often she may say she doesn't (or act like she doesn't). Maintaining that positive attachment will go a long way. Sometimes, bridging the communication gap is the only hurdle, and once you're back on track, you can continue to help her develop into a mature, self-aware, and well-disciplined adult.

Encourage Your Daughter to Spend Time with Friends

It's important that your daughter spend time with others, no matter how social or antisocial she is. Playing and spending time with friends is a crucial part of all children's development, no matter how old they are. However, a CD child may often feel nervous about being with friends in a large social gathering.

Encourage normal outings and parties, and if she doesn't want to do these things, ask her why. Be positive about the outing and ask her what fun thing she would like to do instead. Ask her about her worries and truly listen to them. Her concerns are valid.

Your daughter's main role model is you. If she sees you being overly worried about being around others, she may pick up on that. If you, yourself, are a CD and are trying to encourage your daughter to be more sociable, please lead by example. Get outside your comfort zone and be positive.

Socialize as a Family

According to the American Psychological Association, social skills are learned abilities. It means that you learn how to interact appropriately in different situations. These include things such as making friends, resolving conflicts, communicating, and regulating feelings and behavior.

When children begin school, being social becomes a building block to the foundation of their development. Help your daughter hone these skills before they even get to school. And work on them outside of the classroom with the help of the rest of the family. Doing so will allow your daughter to understand:

- How to cope with disappointment.

- Showing emotion in a healthy manner.

- How to respond to people.

- Taking turns and sharing.

- Body language.

- Listening without interrupting.

- Playing fairly, according to rules and guidelines.

- Accepting the principle "win some, lose some."

- Using appropriate manners and greetings.

Since your first teachers were your parents, what better way to show your daughter how to socialize? Since it is beneficial to lead by example, allowing your daughter to be in your company when you socialize will be an excellent tool.

Be intentional with your teaching and make it activity-based and hands-on. Allow your child the opportunity to really take control of the situation if she wants to and socialize to her heart's content.

Character Play or Make-Believe

Get the toys out, and have your daughter play out scenarios, pretending to be that character. This is usually a child's first socialization exercise.

Taking Turns

Even for those who only have one child, you can still practice taking turns with your children. Take out a toy you know that they love (their favorite or even one that only gets used on special occasions) and have them use it for a few minutes and then tell them their turn is over, and it's your turn (or if you do have other children, then theirs).

Playing Board Games

This is great for the entire family and an obvious way to help practice and encourage social skills within your family. Playing a game with family requires a lot of social skills, including:

- Taking turns.
- Patience.
- Negotiations (which game piece you are or who goes first).
- Following rules.
- Being a good sport ("win some, lose some").

Telling Short Stories

The skills practiced with this exercise include listening, patience, taking turns, and ignoring distractions. It can also aid them in learning empathy.

First, create a stack of flashcards with story topics you might like to discuss with your daughter. Some ideas could include:

- Favorite vacation memory.
- Favorite holiday surprise.
- The best birthday party idea.
- A dream you once had.

Decide who goes first, pick a card, set a timer (two to five minutes), and tell your story. After your daughter tells you her story, it is critical that you show you actively listened to her. Summarize what she said and ask for clarification if you didn't understand something. You can also empathize with her if there was a part in the story that sounded like she was confused, sad, upset, angry, or scared.

Eat Meals Together

Eating together as a family can often lead to great conversation and bonding time with your daughter. Encourage everyone to put their phones or other devices away and simply enjoy each other's company over a nice, warm meal. Mealtime is also a great opportunity for you to teach your daughter the importance of a healthy and balanced diet, which also affects her overall mental health.

Support and Praise Independence

As parents, one of your primary parenting goals is to teach your children how to be independent. One day, your kids will move out of your houses and make their own families. It is the primary responsibility of parents to ensure they're ready and capable of doing so. But it's not always a simple feat.

At times, it's difficult for parents to let go, and in turn, the children become less likely to be self-sufficient and responsible. Some of this is because your instinct as parents is often to make things easier for them, rescuing them from their mistakes.

However, children need to be challenged in order to develop the skills, tenacity, grit, and self-reliance needed to function in the real world on their own. By rescuing your daughter, you will limit her experiences and, in turn, cause more struggles in the future.

It will take time, effort, and a lot of trust, but it is important that you allow your child to become more independent and even praise her when she does so successfully.

Let Your Daughter Make Mistakes

It may seem counterintuitive at first, but just as Chapter 3 states, letting your children make mistakes will teach them how to succeed in life by becoming learning opportunities. When your daughter makes a mistake, it's okay to let it happen. Just make sure you let her know it's okay that it happened, reassure her that it's normal, and help her brainstorm ways that she might prevent making the same one next time. Always treat mistakes as learning opportunities.

Involve Her in Household Tasks

This can start as early as your child is able. For example, teaching your toddler how to get her own cup or straw and then how to pour her own drink is a beginning to independence. Praise her for a job well done.

Encourage her to clean up after herself, help you put away groceries, or pick up her toys. This teaches responsibility, accountability, and independence. Just make sure the chores and tasks you give her are age-appropriate.

Offer Choices and Freedom

Offer your daughter a little bit of freedom (age-appropriately). It's a great way to empower her, build her confidence, and help build a sense of responsibility. This can start young, as well. Even allowing your daughter to pick out her own clothes gives her a bit of freedom and helps her feel more independent. When she's older, and you live in a safe and appropriate distance, consider letting her walk home from school with a friend.

When children can make their own choices, there are more significant opportunities for them to think on the fly and experience the natural consequences of their actions. This is when making mistakes really comes into play. Ultimately, the more practice your daughter has in making choices for herself, the better. But keep in mind that if you provide her with too many options, she might get overwhelmed. So, consider giving her choices rather than letting her make up her mind completely on her own.

Allow Your Daughter the Privacy She Deserves

Most of you have heard the statement "a privilege, not a right," but there is a certain level of privacy that your daughter needs in order to thrive and be successful. The amount your daughter needs is completely subjective to you, your family, and her needs directly. But it should be considered. The key to finding a healthy balance in this area is to set the right expectations, especially where her social life is concerned. For instance, if you give your daughter a cell phone, consider giving her privacy but also setting the expectation that you can check her social media accounts and messages at any time. Or when she uses the computer, her door needs to be open.

Consider allowing her to have something that you won't go through. Diaries or journals are excellent outlets, and if you don't look at it, it could give your daughter a great way to process life without being afraid of what you'll find out.

Offer Additional Support When Needed

If your daughter has any issues with socialization, whether she is a CD or an MY, offer her additional support along the way. You, as her parent, modeling socialization usually goes a long way.

If you feel you have done all you can to support your daughter and her engagement with others and she doesn't seem to be interested, no matter what you try, it may be time to discuss it with a counselor or healthcare provider.

Key Takeaways

Understanding and accommodating your daughter's social needs, whether she's a CD or MY, is crucial for the well-being of not only her but everyone in the family. However, balancing the social lives of everyone in the family is an ongoing process and requires open communication.

Encourage your daughter to express her social preferences, whether it's solitude she seeks or social engagement. Share your feelings and encourage her to compromise if her socialization preferences don't match yours or those of others in the family. Explain that diverse activities can be enriching.

However, understand that there are certain boundaries that you need to have in place. Listen to your daughter's needs where her personal space is concerned and respect the boundaries she asks for. However, if she is a CD, sometimes these boundaries need to be negotiated. Otherwise, she will likely not ever move outside of her comfort zone.

- **Allow Her to Communicate When She Needs Solitude.** Use this time to engage in social interactions if you or other family members are MYs.

- **Maintain a Balanced Social Calendar.** Dedicate specific times for social engagements and personal reflection to validate everyone's needs.

Encourage your daughter to be independent by allowing her to make age-appropriate choices. However, when you do this, make sure you:

- Respect her choices—even if you don't agree with them.

- Allow her to make mistakes.

- Praise her independence.

By navigating social needs, promoting open communication, and respecting personal boundaries, you can strengthen your parent-daughter bond, promote independence, and support her in becoming a well-rounded, self-aware, and responsible adult in the future.

Chapter Five

A Quest for Balance

Going on a quest for balance in your relationship with your CD or MY child can be overwhelming at first, especially if they differ drastically from you or someone else in your immediate family. However, it is important to understand that her emotional strengths are central to her identity and her spot in your family.

In Chapter 5, we explore the art of offering emotional support to MYs during their social endeavors and also understanding CDs in their introspective moments.

You'll learn to navigate conflicts and conflicts that may arise, guiding your daughter on effective emotional regulation and communication. Regular check-ins will help you recognize what your daughter is feeling and how each of you feels you are navigating your emotional roles in your relationship. This chapter will equip you with the tools to validate your daughter, show her how to properly regulate emotionally, and provide excellent communication every step of the way. By the end, you'll be adept at maintaining the delicate balance required for a fulfilling parent-child relationship.

Celebrate the Emotional Strengths Each Type Brings to the Family

Celebrating the emotional strengths each personality type can bring to the family is essential. This especially helps where your children are concerned. It will allow for bonding and growth with your daughter and resonate with her emotionally.

Identify Emotional Strengths and Compliment Them

Take the time to identify and acknowledge the unique emotional strengths each person in your family has. CDs often bring introspection, empathy, and stability, while MYs may contribute enthusiasm, spontaneity, and optimism. Recognize how your emotional strengths complement your family, including your daughter, and vice versa.

CDs can provide a stabilizing presence during challenging times, while MYs can infuse energy and positivity into familial relationships where negativity could quickly take over. Personality strengths are part of people's identity and are ingrained in them rather than learned. Some people have natural gifts. Learn to appreciate these differences because each of you can lean on one another during times of difficulty. Be sure that you do this in an age-appropriate manner, though. Don't put too much emotional pressure on your young child. Instead, save some of this for a time when your daughter is emotionally mature.

Express Gratitude

Regardless of age, though, you can regularly express your gratitude for your daughter and the emotional strengths she possesses and brings to the table. Sometimes, your children are great at pinpointing if you have had a particularly rough day, and if you notice that your daughter attempts to help you feel better, show her gratitude to her. A simple "Thank you" can go a long way.

Offer Emotional Support to MYs in Their Social Endeavors and Understand CDs in Their Introspective Moments

Offer Support to MYs in Their Social Endeavors

We have spoken about MYs and their social endeavors. But remember, by supporting your daughter in what she is drawn to, such as her social endeavors, you are strengthening the emotional bond between you. Ways to support and encourage those endeavors include:

- Encouraging her attendance at parties and celebrating her for the social butterfly she is.

- Actively participating in social events and outings with her or allowing her to go without you when the occasion calls and she has earned the trust.

- Respecting her independence and the time she sets aside for friends.

- Planning surprise parties for her.

Understand and Listen to CDs in Their Introspective Moments

Understanding your CD daughter during her introspective moments is essential to building a strong and empathetic connection with her. Here's how to navigate these reflective periods:

- Respect her need for solitude and create a supportive environment for her to be alone.

- Practice patience—don't rush her into doing things that make them uncomfortable.

- Validate her emotions.

- Avoid judgment.

- Respect her privacy.

- Express your availability to talk whenever she is ready.

Understanding and listening to your CD daughter, especially during times of reflection, shows that you are a supportive parent. You can truly build a stronger and longer-lasting bond with her by creating a safe and nonjudgmental space for her to flourish.

Conflicts Will Arise—Show Your Daughter How to Handle Them

No one likes dealing with conflict. But no matter how hard you try to avoid it, arguments, fights, and disagreements are a fact of life—for adults and for children.

Conflict may not be pleasant, but it doesn't have to feel catastrophic. Teaching kids practical skills to manage it in a healthy way will help them navigate everything from small arguments to big ones.

Part of what makes conflicts difficult to navigate is the way they bring out big, intense emotions. Children have to learn how to not only recognize these big emotions but how to process them as well.

Parents should always start by helping children identify emotions. Emotion charts help with this tremendously and can be given at very early ages to help kids recognize what emotion they may be feeling.

While your daughter's emotions are heightened, it's best to help her regulate first. She doesn't have to completely understand the issue immediately, but she will need to be calm in the heat of the moment.

Help her discover what works best for her to keep her calm—something in her emotional tool belt that will help her regulate. This can be a pet, a calm-down nook, deep breaths, or even just splashing cool water on her face. Anything that works. Once she's calm, she can start working on dealing with the issue itself.

Pinpoint the Source of the Conflict

Once big emotions have cooled down, the next step is figuring out exactly what the problem is. Sometimes kids, especially younger ones, don't have the emotional awareness to identify the original source of the conflict. They might need your help to understand why they're feeling whatever it is that they are feeling.

Helping your daughter get to the root of the issue will make it easier for her to resolve the issue. It will also give her tools to identify and talk about similar problems when they come up again. Older kids in grade school and middle school are more likely to have the language to identify the source of the conflict, so with a little guidance, they can learn to use these skills independently going forward. Younger children may require a bit more patience to get to the root of everything.

Brainstorm Solutions Together

Once your daughter understands what the issue is, you can help her practice finding solutions. The younger the child, the more guidance they will need, but even your teenage daughter will benefit from your input.

Recognize and Validate Your Daughter's Feelings through Regular Check-Ins

Regular relationship check-ins provide a platform to address concerns and strengthen your connection with your daughter. These can be as often as you need them to be. Some families do them every night, some once a week, and some may only check in once a month. Do what works best for you and your daughter. It may take a little time to find that perfect sweet spot, too, so don't be afraid to include her and ask if she feels you are checking in enough.

Pick a Regular Time

Ideally, you'll both be relaxed, present, and in a good mood, so don't schedule a check-in after a long day at work or when you're short of time. You want to bring your best attitude and a clear mindset to these meetings with your daughter.

Set the Scene

Your relationship check-in is an opportunity to slow down and connect, so why not make it feel a little special? To that end, bring your favorite snacks and drinks—and conduct the check-in somewhere that feels good to both of you. It needs to be a private and secluded atmosphere, so you both feel comfortable delving into your emotions. Ordering takeout and planning something relaxing to do afterward can also help set the scene and feel like a great reward or incentive.

Celebrate and Appreciate Her

Always start with positives. This appreciation gives your daughter peace when it comes to sharing things with you. Giving compliments and joyful feedback upfront helps your daughter feel comfortable and valued. This is especially necessary if there are more challenging topics to discuss afterward. Appreciation and validation are essential ingredients for a quality relationship with your daughter.

Always Finish on a High Point

A celebration, even a small one, can be a fun way to wrap up the check-in. Remember, these check-ins aren't meant to regurgitate everything your daughter has done wrong. It's a great time to bring up something that is consistently an issue, but only after you discuss her positives. After all, you should be having conversations about issues or wrongdoings as they happen. This is merely a time to check in on how she is doing, let her know how you're doing (or the rest of the family), and if there are still adjustments to be made. If you wait to vent during these check-ins, and these check-ins alone, you may be a powder keg next to an open flame—ready to explode! You definitely don't want that. Your daughter needs to trust that your check-ins are safe places.

Also, remember to end the session with a physical touch or an affirmation of love and appreciation. Even if things get a little tense or something feels unresolved, find a way to come back to discuss them later.

Show Her Firsthand What Emotional Regulation and Effective Communication Look Like

As discussed previously with conflicts, it's important that you help your child find tools that work for them to regulate their emotions. If you're a parent, chances are you've witnessed a tantrum at least once. You expect them in two-year-olds. But if your child reaches school age and meltdowns and outbursts are still frequent, it may be a sign that they have difficulty with emotional self-regulation.

What Is Self-Regulation

Self-regulation is the ability to understand and manage your behavior and your reactions to feelings and things happening around you. It includes being able to resist highly emotional reactions to upsetting situations, to calm yourself down when you get upset, and to handle frustration without an outburst.

Emotional Dysregulation

Problems with self-regulation manifest in different ways depending on the person. This mostly happens in children but can happen in adults as well. If you have issues with self-regulation, it is recommended you speak to a counselor so that you can lead by example with your daughter.

Some individuals have instantaneous and strong reactions (usually a blow-up) with no lead-in or build-up. Others have a continuous build-up, and it progresses until they can't handle it anymore—which causes an outburst.

Why Do Some Kids Struggle with Self-Regulation

This is generally a combination of temperament and learned behaviors. Generally, babies who have difficulties self-soothing are more likely to have emotional self-regulation issues.

However, the environment can play a huge role. When parents give in to tantrums or work overtime to soothe their children when they get upset, children will often use their parents to regulate them.

Children with ADHD or anxiety may find it particularly challenging to manage their emotions and need more help to develop emotional regulation skills.

Teach Your Daughter Self-Regulation Skills

The key to learning self-regulation skills is not to avoid situations that are difficult for your daughter to handle. This can be challenging, especially if she is struggling, but it is important not to "save the day."

Instead, coach her through the situation and provide as much support as she needs to get through it herself.

Imagine a situation that can produce strong negative emotions, like a frustrating math homework assignment. If a parent hovers too much, they risk taking over the regulation role. Either your daughter might rely on you to fix the situation by helping her with every single problem, or she may think the frustration she's feeling is because of you—since you're the one making her do the homework in the first place and you're the one hanging around so closely.

Instead of giving in and helping her with all the problems, the best method is to help her with *one of them*. Show her how to do it, and then let her try. If she still feels frustrated, encourage her to take a break and go grab a drink to decompress for a moment. Suggest for her to even use a timer to give herself periodic breaks, too, and let her know that you will check in on her at certain intervals. When you do, be sure to give her praise for all of her hard work.

By showing her how to tackle the issue, and then offering her breaks away from the situation when she gets overwhelmed, you are teaching her how to regulate her emotions. This comes in handy when bigger situations arise later down the road.

Transitioning

Many young children have difficulty with what is known as "transitioning," i.e., when they are asked to stop one activity and move on to another activity (generally one a little less appealing). For example, if your daughter is playing a video game and you ask her to finish the game to get ready for bed, it's likely she will feel frustrated and upset.

When she's feeling these big emotions, sometimes it's difficult to know how to regulate them. If your daughter is prone to melting down when asked to stop one activity and move on to the next, consider practicing transitions.

Dry Run Practice

Dry runs are another way to teach self-regulation. For instance, if you've had trouble with a child reacting impulsively or having a tantrum in a store or during a transition, consider practicing ways to make this situation easier on your child—and you.

For instance, if your daughter throws tantrums in the grocery store, consider taking her with you on a short visit when you don't need to do serious shopping. Have her practice walking with you, keeping her hands to herself, and even consider making a game out of it and giving her points when she is successful.

If your daughter is the type to get upset after being asked to get off the video games and go brush her teeth, consider giving her a countdown to the video game shutoff time and have a conversation beforehand about regulating. Practice this before the actual "toothbrushing" scenario with other events. For example, while she's playing her game, give her a countdown. Tell her in five minutes she will need to get off the game and walk to the kitchen for a drink (or something similar). Continue this every minute until five minutes are up. After she has successfully transitioned from her video game to walking to the kitchen, you can try to incorporate the toothbrushing scenario once again. Make sure that you praise her good work throughout this experience. Remember, it's easy to get discouraged when things don't go well, but skill-building is all about consistency. Don't give up. Just try to knock down the activity, so it's more doable, and slowly give your child more and more independence to handle it the way you expect them to.

Key Takeaways

It is important to recognize and celebrate the unique emotional strengths that each family member, including your daughter, brings to the family. CDs may offer introspection and stability, while MYs contribute enthusiasm and optimism.

Express gratitude to your daughter and show her how much you appreciate and respect her:

- Remember, a "Thank you" can go a long way in showing her that you respect and care for her individuality and the emotional strengths she brings to the table.

- Encourage and support her in her social activities and even participate in them with her.

- Be sensitive to her need for solitude by creating a supportive environment that respects her privacy and validates her emotions.

It is also critical to teach your daughter that conflicts are a part of life and that you teach her resolution skills that will help her navigate disagreements and arguments in a healthy way. Great ways to explore these at younger ages include emotion charts to pinpoint the feelings of those around her.

Help her identify emotions as well as root causes of conflicts—and be prepared to brainstorm solutions together to fix conflicts as they arise.

And finally, make sure you are engaging in regular relationship check-ins with your daughter and that you follow these rules:

- Be consistent.
- Start with positive feedback.
- Celebrate her achievements.
- Finish on a high note.

Remember, these check-ins are not the place to vent frustrations; they are opportunities to strengthen your bond.

Model emotional regulation and effective communication for your daughter during these check-ins and outside of them. This will help her identify and manage strong feelings. Encourage her to use emotional tools and self-regulation strategies that work for her and encourage her to find what those are by becoming self-reflective.

Chapter Six

Establishing Healthy Boundaries

In Chapter 6, we delve into the importance of establishing healthy boundaries for your CD and MY daughters. Creating boundaries is essential to your daughter's development.

For CD daughters, the focus will be on providing space and quiet time, recognizing her preference for introspection. And for MYs, we will work on fostering her desire for adventure and self-expression and how to use this to give her freedom and independence.

This chapter also guides you on respecting your daughter's autonomy by seeking her input and consent before offering advice, and it's about understanding that every child is different and deserves personalized boundaries to thrive.

Create Boundaries *with* Your Daughter

Boundaries are an important part of creating clarity between you and your daughter. By setting and agreeing on boundaries together, you create a "contract" of expected behavior. This behavior is the standard to avoid conflict. While boundaries help parents feel more in control of their child's behavior, they also help the child by:

- Letting her know that you care about her.
- Making her feel safe and supported.
- Helping her make informed and sound decisions.
- Providing her a foundation for which she has autonomy.

Prior to discussing boundaries with your daughter, sit down with your partner and/or all of the important authority figures for your daughter and agree on what the most important boundaries are. It's crucial that there is a general consensus between everyone to ensure that you are all giving clear and firm boundaries—rather than mixed signals and messages. Discuss items such as:

- What are the most important boundaries?
- Which boundaries are negotiable, and which are not?
- What kind of consequences are you comfortable with if she crosses the boundaries?
- At what age do the boundaries change?

All these questions can apply to a variety of behaviors as well as various ages. Boundaries are always important to establish, even when your child is a toddler. But creating them with your daughter, after gaining input from other adults in her life, creates a great atmosphere for trust. Some of the major examples you will likely discuss as a parent of a teenager include things like going out with friends, going to parties, sexual experimentation, drinking, and social media use.

These conversations can be incredibly difficult, but make sure you engage with your daughter and give her an opportunity to speak. Use active listening and truly pay attention to her. There are two different ways you can approach boundary setting with your daughter. You can choose to sit down with her to discuss boundaries around a variety of issues, or you can choose to set boundaries as she requests more freedom, one at a time.

Regardless of which direction you find yourself going in, it's important to choose a good time of day to have the discussion. Make sure you have plenty of time (for questions and clarity), that you're both in a relatively good mood, and that there's not been any recent conflict (if she thinks you're upset with her, she may think that your boundaries are harsh and a direct representation of what she has done wrong). Ideally, have the discussion with the whole family present.

When setting boundaries with your daughter, it's important to get her feedback and input into the process. Young people are less likely to adhere to boundaries that have been dictated to them without any sort of negotiation at all. So, let her have some input.

If the conversation leads to conflict, suggest taking a break and follow up when things have cooled down a bit. Also, try not to overload the conversation with too many boundaries all at once. Again, suggest a follow-up talk to cover additional things—or other things that come up later.

A good way to finish up a boundary-setting conversation is to ask your daughter what boundaries she would like you to stick to. This conversation can be very enlightening and can help to bring mutual understanding and respect between you. Let your daughter know that you want to teach her how to set boundaries for herself, and make sure you are one of the first to show her what respecting those boundaries looks like. Because even though she is your daughter, just like the boundaries that you provide for her, it's important that you stick to those that she provides for you when it comes to her autonomy.

Consequences

The process of setting boundaries is one that will likely need to be repeated fairly often during the teenage years. Not only are you giving them more freedoms and responsibilities, loosening some boundaries, but there may also be situations that arise where you restrict some boundaries already in place.

Boundaries may also need to be shifted if your child exhibits untrustworthy behavior. More restrictions can be a consequence of ignoring or crossing lines.

Don't Lose Hope

Testing boundaries is normal teenage behavior. No matter how good your relationship is with your child or how good your daughter is, she will still cross some boundaries.

There can be several reasons behind this:

- Impulsive behavior.
- The influence of their peers.
- Plain ol' poor decision-making.

As parents, you have a responsibility to invest in, care for, and equip your daughters, and in many cases that is setting boundaries.

Teaching your daughter how to set boundaries gives her an opportunity to have input and partner with you. You are still the parent, and you have the authority, ultimately, but don't be afraid to let her in on some of the rules. Of course, she will likely try to slide one past you. Do not let her set her own curfew, skip school, or make up rules. Instead, involve her in the process.

Explain That Boundaries Are Made with Love

Many times, your children look at rules and think they are a form of punishment when it's actually protection. A great way to explain this to your daughter, at any age, is in reference to the lines on a road. There are lines—boundaries—that keep you safely in your lane. If you venture outside of those lanes, whether intentionally or unintentionally, you open yourself up to the potential of a great risk. You need boundaries to keep you safe.

A great boundary to set up with your teenager is the curfew. It isn't recommended she make up her own curfew, but asking her what she thinks is a reasonable curfew time can help get the ball rolling on the conversation. This will open up negotiations. Ultimately, she just wants to be heard and feel as though she has an influence. Give her that.

Give Your CD Space and Quiet Time

Respect Her Need for Solitude

CDs often cherish alone time. A considerate surprise could involve giving her the gift of solitude. Plan an evening out with your partner or even just retire to another part of the house to give your daughter some likely much-needed personal time.

Book a Relaxing Retreat

Research secluded cabins in nature where you can all go to disconnect from the daily grind. Make sure there are amenities that you all enjoy there, such as a nice fireplace you can sit next to (maybe even roast marshmallows), a pool table you can shoot pool on while she reads out on the porch, or even a hot tub everyone can relax in and enjoy quality time together. Surprising her with a weekend escape might be exactly what she needs to recharge.

Create a Personalized Reading Nook

If your CD daughter enjoys reading, surprise her by setting up a personalized reading nook in your home. Choose a comfortable chair, add soft and warm lighting, and stock it with her favorite books or magazines (extra points if you add an area for some tasty snacks).

Go on a Stargazing Adventure

Plan a stargazing night in a remote location away from city lights. Bring a telescope if you want a closer look, but the naked eye can capture the moment as well. Don't forget your daughter's favorite snacks and some drinks to make a full night of it away from the hustle and bustle. This is great for the entire family.

Foster Your MY's Desire for Adventure and Expression

Surprise Party with Friends

If your MY daughter enjoys socializing, plan a surprise party with some of her closest friends and your family. Coordinate with your loved ones to ensure everyone can attend, and keep it a secret until the big reveal. MYs love surprises!

Adventure Getaway

Surprise her with an adventurous weekend getaway. Choose destinations that offer exciting experiences like hiking a rigorous trail, zip-lining, rock-climbing wall, exploring a new city, and if she is particularly adventurous—add in a helicopter ride or something equally as thrilling! MYs often find excitement in new and dynamic environments.

Something to Wear

MYs love attention. Buying her a special gift—whether that be that beautiful dress she's been eyeing for the dance or nice flashy jewelry, it's sure to impress her, and complimenting her while she wears it will make her feel even better about herself.

Respect Your Daughter's Needs and Wants

It is important that you discuss your daughter's needs and wants periodically with her. Start this discussion at your regular check-ins. Ask her what she wants out of life and what she feels like she needs to be fulfilled.

This is generally a conversation for a mentally and emotionally mature child but can be altered to fit a younger child. Children of all ages have needs and wants. Respecting those is crucial to obtaining and keeping your daughter's trust.

Encourage Her to Share Her Feelings

After you've expressed your thoughts and feelings, encourage her to do the same. Ensure that she feels safe and supported in sharing her wants and needs with you. When she speaks, ensure you are practicing active listening. This means giving her your full attention, maintaining eye contact, and showing empathy. Avoid interrupting or passing judgment—no matter where the conversation leads. Ask open-ended questions to gain a deeper understanding of her perspective.

Address Concerns Respectfully

Address any concern you have with what your daughter shares with you. Avoid becoming defensive or dismissive. Instead, acknowledge her feelings and work together to find solutions or compromises that respect what she needs and her emotions.

Respect Boundaries

While you are communicating with your daughter, it is essential to recognize that boundaries are important. If she is not comfortable with discussing certain things with you yet, then—no matter how difficult it is—respect her boundaries and give her space. You can revisit the topic when she is ready.

Ask before Giving Advice

As a parent, it is difficult not to give advice at the drop of a hat when it comes to your children. It is difficult not to feel completely like it's your job to "fix" things when they are troubling your daughter. Next time your daughter comes to you to vent, take a deep breath, slow down, and ask something like this: "Do you want to just tell me how you feel, or do you want advice?"

Obviously, as her parent, you're going to have your own opinion, but sometimes your daughter just wants to talk. She doesn't want advice at all—and she definitely doesn't want you to fix it. If this is her desire, respect that. No matter how frustrating it is. No matter how simple the fix may be.

Sometimes, she will want advice—wait for those moments. The advice will mean more to her when that time comes, and it will honestly mean more to you, knowing that it was something she asked for.

Key Takeaways

Boundaries are crucial for setting expectations and avoiding conflicts with your daughter. They convey your care, support, and the importance of informed decision-making. Discuss and agree on the most important boundaries with other authority figures in your daughter's life, such as your partner, to ensure consistency in the messages everyone conveys.

Although it may be difficult, be prepared to discuss various boundary topics, such as going out with friends, parties, sexual experimentation, drinking, and social media use, depending on your daughter's age.

Involve your daughter in the process of setting boundaries, giving her a voice and ownership in the decisions she makes. Encourage a cooperative and respectful tone throughout the conversation. Make sure she knows this isn't a way to get what she wants but to gain more responsibility by having a chance to discuss boundaries with you before you set them.

Explain that boundaries are based on love and protection, not punishment, and set this expectation at a young age. Use examples to illustrate how boundaries serve as safeguards for young children.

Remember that setting a boundary is not a one-time task. They will evolve as your daughter grows up. Also, recognize that teenagers will test boundaries, and while frustrating, it is a normal part of their development. When this happens, remind them of the agreed-upon rules, ask them to identify how they broke your rule, and jointly decide on consequences. Always make sure to follow through with those consequences.

Setting boundaries alongside your daughter gives her a dose of what it can be like for her in the future. But it doesn't always have to be the future where she sets her own boundaries. Here is a list of ways to develop a sense of autonomy for your daughter:

- Adhere to boundaries she places on you (if reasonable).

- Encourage her to place boundaries on others.

- Respect her needs and her choices.
- Respond with empathy.
- Ask before giving advice.

Remember, setting and respecting boundaries is an ongoing process that helps guide your daughter toward responsible behavior and adulthood. Encourage mutual respect, open communication, and understanding in this journey.

Chapter Seven

Have Fun

Remember back to your childhood. Hopefully, the memories are fond and playful. Regardless, though, it is likely you understand how essential it is for your daughter to have fun and play. Play allows children to learn and develop and gives their brains positive stimulation to thrive.

Chapter 7 is all about just that—having fun! Not only having fun, though, but also creating lasting memories with your CD and MY daughters.

After all, fun is a universal language of love and bonding. In this chapter, we explore various activities, including quieter ones for CDs that respect their need for solitude. On the flip side, we also discuss how to embrace the high-energy spirit of MYs and encourage you to play with your child—a lot.

It is important to build a deeper connection with your daughter through laughter. Use these guidelines to help you discover the joy of making memories by engaging in activities that your CD or MY love most.

By the end of this chapter, you'll be equipped to create a fun and loving environment at home filled with laughter, memorable moments, and cherished experiences that will last a lifetime.

Do Quiet Activities with Your CD

It is important that if you have a CD child, you invest time in doing quiet activities with them. Make sure that you aren't exceeding the threshold they have for outside stimulation. CDs can be sensitive to crowds and people; it is very important not to push them too hard. Allow them some time to process their experiences before moving on to the next one. Observe your daughter's body language during group activities and other social situations, and help her escape if you see that her social battery has been drained.

You can do this in a lot of different ways. For example, you can suggest that she go read a good book that she may not be familiar with or offer a word game or puzzle—and even possibly see if she would like to do this activity together. Excuse yourselves if necessary and go enjoy alone time together.

If she wants complete solitude, respect that, but try again later. Doing quiet activities with her may be what she needs to feel connected with you once again, but she may need to recharge first.

A fun, ongoing activity you can enjoy with your CD daughter is becoming her pen pal. Write letters to one another throughout her youth. This is a great way to get creative juices flowing and also offer a genuine way for your daughter to open up to you without feeling the pressure of doing it in person, vocally.

Provide Opportunities for Creative Expression throughout the Day

This is a simple way to reach your CD daughter while also encouraging and building on an area of natural strength. CD children are often innovative. Exposing her to art, music, science, literature, or various physical activities can be very positive for her.

Allow her to have her private space, especially if she has her own bedroom. If you are in a loud household, set aside some quiet time during the day to help her recharge.

Encourage Your CD to Spend Time with Family or Friends

Let your daughter participate in solitary activities at times, especially when she is feeling overstimulated. Do not force her to interact with family members or guests until she feels ready. However, always encourage her to spend time with the rest of the family and jump outside of her comfort zone every once in a while.

It's important in doing this that you reassure her that she can take a break when she needs one. Teach her words that she can use to excuse herself from the group and have a retreat area already in mind that she can go to for some alone time.

It's important to discuss some of this beforehand, especially if you're in a new environment. If you are taking your CD child to a family member's house that she is unfamiliar with, make sure that you have a plan in place with your daughter as well as the host (your family member).

If your CD daughter is spending time with the family, respect the courage it takes. Make sure you are being patient and going through experiences at a relaxed pace at first. Doing this will show your daughter it is safe to open up because you respect her boundaries.

You play an important role in helping your CD daughter embrace her inner self. Since CDs energize by being with themselves, your child may need some time to process her experiences and feelings before she can talk about what she is thinking. But make sure she comes back together with the family once she's recharged.

Do Independent Activities near Your CD, Such as Reading or Art

Bonding with your CD may look a little different from what you imagined when you first found out you were having a child. While all CDs differ from each other slightly, with their own individual personalities, generally speaking, they ultimately prefer quiet and intimate surroundings.

While you can still have fun and play with your CD daughter, make sure you are setting time aside to just be near them without interacting a whole lot socially. Reading a book nearby, painting a portrait, or even doing a puzzle will allow you an opportunity to sit in silence with your CD daughter. This will give you both opportunities for reflection but also allow your CD daughter to feel close to you.

Allow Your CD to Plan What You Do Together

Whenever in doubt about how your CD daughter is feeling emotionally, knowing just how full her social battery is, allow her to plan what you do together during your special time together.

Not only are you fulfilling a need of a CD—by allowing her to be in control of the situation—you're also respecting her desire to do whatever her heart is aching to do. This creates a bonding experience as it shows her that you trust her to make a decision for both of you. This in turn helps your daughter trust *you*.

Inspire Your MY to Try New Things

MYs are notoriously adventurous. This can be an absolutely wonderful thing, and by encouraging her to try new things, you can open up a whole world to her!

Teach Her How to Assess Risk

If your daughter is an MY, chances are she likes adventure. Before she goes on these adventures, though, it's important to learn how to assess risk. Children experience a thrill and master fears through "risky" activities like tree climbing or sledding. By doing these sorts of activities, they learn to face fears and take control of situations.

If your daughter wants to do certain activities and is worried about it, reassure her that you have looked into the safety factors and would not put her in a situation that was dangerous.

Discuss how you arrived at this decision from an early age. Some activities have a higher risk of getting hurt. Safety measures like wearing a helmet or elbow and knee pads prevent her from getting hurt. Discuss why she wears those because it will give her a sense of duty to always know the safety factors before involving herself in these kinds of adventurous or thrilling activities.

Don't Pressure

Although it's great to show your daughter new thrilling activities or sports, make sure that you're not pressuring her. While trying experiences such as these can help her face fears, make sure she is actually the one choosing to participate—and it isn't just you thinking she might want to because she's an MY. Every child is unique and has their own preferences for activities. Encourage your daughter, but don't pressure her.

Next Steps Lead to New Adventures

When your daughter masters one thing, see if she wants to try something new. If she does, then consider having her try the next step up. For example:

- If she has tried sledding, have her try snowboarding or skiing.
- If she has tried a Ferris wheel, have her try a roller coaster.
- If she has tried a ropes course, have her try zip-lining.
- If she has tried the monkey bars, have her try climbing a tree.
- If she has tried biking, have her try mountain biking.
- If she has tried skateboarding on the sidewalk, have her try skateboarding at the skate park.
- If she has tried canoeing or kayaking, have her try river rafting.

Incorporate Plenty of Social Interaction for Your MY in Her Daily Life

There are plenty of ways to incorporate a little more social interaction in your daughter's daily life. However, encouraging social endeavors that are positive will help your daughter develop positive and healthy relationships for the future.

- **Model Good Friendship Skills:** Children learn from seeing. Make sure you have good friends and act positively with your friends in front of her.

- **Encourage the Friendships That Are Important to Your Child:** If your daughter has a best friend, make sure that you're allowing them to spend a lot of time together.

- **Ask About Friends and Plan Playdates:** When children are very young, it's sometimes difficult for them to communicate with their friends and then you about wanting to play with their friends at school or preschool. If you find that your daughter is talking about the same kid at school often, it's likely this is their best friend. Try to coordinate with your daughter's friend's parents and get them together outside of school.

- **Respect Your Child's Personality and Interests:** All children differ, even if they hold the same personality types as another. Make sure that you're respecting your child's personality as well as her interests. If she likes dance or gymnastics, have her be involved in a local class with children her age. This could create friendships, but at the very least, she's doing something she enjoys.

- **Emphasize the Importance of Staying Connected:** Model this and stay connected to your friends and family. Let your daughter know that staying connected to the people you love is healthy for your minds and bodies.

- **Model Empathy and Compassion:** Your daughter will understand this more fully after she's grown up in an environment where you model this behavior, especially when talking with her. Make sure you listen to your daughter actively, and show her that you care about what she's talking about.

- **Encourage Your Child to Start New Friendships and Maintain Existing Ones:** This can sometimes be a juggling act for adults. This is a great skill to learn and practice often. It teaches your daughter how to manage her time and her friends appropriately—while also considering her own needs.

- **Talk with Your Child About When It Is Appropriate or Necessary to End a Friendship and How to Do So Respectfully:** Everyone has experienced an unhealthy friendship/relationship at one point in their lives. It is important for your daughter to recognize when to walk away. Walking away doesn't always mean not loving someone. It just means that the relationship is no longer healthy. Help her understand and recognize signs of unhealthy relationships.

- **Have Conversations About Bullying and Kindness:** This will teach your daughter to become compassionate and empathetic to others.

The most important of all is to teach her how to become a good friend. Skills learned through her social connections are not only important for her current friendships and life but for all of her future relationships as well.

Embrace Your MY's High-Energy Spirit

MYs are generally high-energy. However, it's crucial to understand your child's energy and when it comes from actual energy or if it's them compensating. Extra energy is sometimes a disguise when they feel frustrated or overwhelmed.

Be curious and make sure you understand if it's her true energy rearing its head or if it's something deeper. A great way to embrace true high energy is to find healthy outlets for your daughter to release energy. Two broad categories of these outlets are:

- **Free Play:** Running around on a playground or engaging in active play, such as a game of tag with friends.

- **Structured Activities:** These are structured activities such as structured sports or ballet classes.

Play with Your MY—A Lot

No matter the age of your daughter, it is crucial that you play! Especially if she's an MY and has higher energy.

How to Play with Your Baby

The time you spend with your baby is the beginning of developing her self-esteem and self-worth. Think of it this way: you are following her lead—and engaging with her in her own world.

Keep It Simple

First things first, when you're playing with a baby, keep it simple. You don't have to buy fancy toys for your baby. Everything is new to them. They will be satisfied with almost anything as long as it is positive.

Have you ever heard the stories about the babies who receive all those big, expensive gifts for Christmas—only to be more interested in the box it came in?

The best way to play with your infant daughter is to just be present and respond to her. When she babbles or coos, talk to her.

Be sure that when you engage with her, though, you're enthusiastic. Giving a smile or a clap will encourage her to remain focused. Studies show that this level of interaction helps develop dopamine levels in her brain, which in turn sets her up to be resilient and interested in learning.

Small little tickles or pokes to your baby's belly or fun songs are another great way to play with your infant daughter. If you move her around while you sing, she will learn what is referred to as "rhythmic movement stimulation," and this is essential for children to learn how to regulate their movements. Starting this early is a great way to set your daughter up for success in learning. Another great idea is to get out textured toys or crinkly books so your daughter can explore different sensory items during play. These can be items from home as well, such as a wooden spoon she can bang against things. It will allow her the opportunity to explore her senses. She will begin to understand the difference between soft and hard and squishy and firm.

Make sure you pay attention to any cues she gives you as a signal she's done playing.

How to Play with Your Toddler

First and foremost with a toddler, stay close by! Your daughter is becoming more independent and developing her own interests, but she will explore in every imaginable way. This can be a particularly difficult stage of life, but it can also be incredibly rewarding.

Some of the best toys you can get your toddler are toys that develop motor skills and help advance problem-solving abilities.

- **Large Puzzles:** These can aid in both of those. Consider taking turns putting the pieces together to show her how first, and then take a step back and let her try. Don't jump in unless she gets frustrated.

- **Building Blocks:** These are wonderful with motor skills too and can help develop brain functionality and development.

- **Kicking Balls Back and Forth:** This is particularly excellent—but only if your daughter is able to walk and stand on her own. This aids in motor skills but also in taking turns and cooperation.

- **Gentle Roughhousing:** A favorite game of many children is being picked up and tossed into the air by their parents and even flown around the living room. This is another example of beneficial play. It will not only strengthen the bond you have with your daughter but also teach her consent.

- **Coloring:** Learning to color is difficult for children. Consider using chunky crayons with your toddler, and at first, let her imagination run wild. Don't worry about her staying in the lines at first. This can come later after she learns how to keep the crayon in her hand without breaking it and keeping the crayon on the sheet of paper.

How to Play with Your Preschooler

This is one of the most exciting times to play with children. This is when kids' imaginations run wild, and they enjoy dressing up or diving into the world of make-believe. Don't be afraid to play pretend with your preschool daughter.

Some other fun activities to play with your preschool-aged daughter include:

- **Flash Card Games:** This is an especially great way to learn letters and shapes.

- **Playdough:** Who doesn't love getting their hands a little dirty? Playdough is one of the best toys for imaginative play and sensory.

- **Handwriting:** Why not get a head start on school and teach your daughter how to write her name? This will set her ahead of the curve and give her a sense of achievement.

- **Coloring:** Coloring is often one of the best activities to do with your children, no matter their age. At preschool age, make sure you hold your daughter to a bit of a higher standard. Ask her to keep it inside the lines for more finesse to her motor skills!

- **Roughhousing:** Don't be afraid to amp up the roughhousing with your preschool-aged child. Play wrestling is a really good sensory activity. Just make sure you establish rules like consent so that she understands when playtime is over, it's over.

Preschoolers ultimately crave attention and feeling like big kids. Let your preschool daughter help you with household tasks and make a game out of it. Matching socks is just as good as a matching-style board game. Not only can she help you out, but she can also feel like a productive member of your household by doing small things like this.

How to Play with Your School-Aged Daughter

Now that your daughter is school-aged, she is likely at a great age to learn and enjoy a lot more activities.

Some great activities to introduce to your school-aged daughter are:

- **Board Games:** School-age children can learn and play by rules. Playing these helps brain development and teaches her how to follow rules and guidelines.

- **Physical Games:** Sports and games like tag are engaging and physical. Playing these kinds of games helps keep your daughter physically stimulated and instills even more rules, including keeping your hands in check. It's easy to keep your hands to yourself during board games; it's another to keep your hands in check during a game of football. Learning appropriate boundaries through games like this is beneficial. Plus, the activity is a great way to burn extra energy and help your daughter feel calm and content.

- **Open-Ended Activities:** Games like LEGO, dolls, or kitchen sets help build an imaginative world with your school-aged child.

- **Video Games:** If your kid is into video games, hanging out and playing them, even if just for a few minutes, will count as playing and will give you a great opportunity to see what it is that they enjoy so much.

Build a Deeper Connection with Your Daughter through Fun and Laughter

Laughing with your kids is special because it builds a bond with them. These moments create a more uplifting environment at home. Laughter tends to be contagious, so before you know it, your whole house could be giggling up a storm if you engage in laughing and playing.

So, how can you laugh more with your kids?

- Start a laughing contest to see who can make the other person laugh first.

- Play fun games like Pictionary, Headbanz, or charades.

- Read joke books, and share your favorites with each other.

- Create funny stories together.

- Have a family talent show and see who comes up with the funniest routine.

- Dress up in silly costumes.

- Watch a comedy television show or movie together as a family.

Make Memories Doing What Your CD or MY Love Most

Sometimes, as parents, you are busy. It's easy to still make memories with your daughter without dedicating an entire day. Even just twenty minutes to enjoy activities together will go a long way with your daughter.

- Blow bubbles outside.

- Ask her to help you with some of the more fun chores around the house.

- Wash the car (this gets chores done and lets you spend fun time with your daughter).

- Pull weeds together.

- Plant flowers—and tell her that they're both of your flowers.

- Play a level of a video game—or even just watch them play. Cheer her on!

Being a kid with your kid allows her to see a fun side of you and feel like the two of you have a lot in common. It also gives her the idea that she matters—and that you matter to her. This can truly inspire childhood memories that your daughter can draw on later. She will look back with fondness and know that she had a great parent (or parents) who cared about her and her needs.

Create Parent-Child Rituals

Make a point of spending individual time with your daughter. Quality, one-on-one time with your daughter can strengthen the parent-child bond as well as build up her self-esteem.

Your daughter needs to feel special and valued. Consider scheduling special "date nights" with your daughter to create that one-on-one opportunity. This can be as small or as big as you want it to be. Take a walk around the park, go to the playground, do dinner and a movie—it doesn't matter. Just celebrate her individually.

When children look back on their childhoods, they rarely remember the expensive gifts or fancy dinners out. They remember their parents' intentions in giving them the gifts and the sacrifices made for them.

Memories are hugely important to build bonds, encourage a lifelong connection, and help keep happiness in your household. Setting aside time for your children will be an action that rewards you for the rest of your life.

Key Takeaways

This chapter emphasizes the importance of having fun with your CD and MY daughters, highlighting the different approaches required for each personality type.

Make sure that you engage in quiet activities with your CD, especially when she requires a bit of recharging. Engage in activities such as:

- Reading.
- Word games.

- Puzzles.

- Writing each other.

Make sure you respect your CD's private space. Make sure she has space inside the home to recharge. Be supportive and understanding and encourage creative expression. CDs are often introspective and do well with innovative activities such as:

- Art.

- Music.

- Science.

- Literature.

When she's fully charged, encourage her to spend time with family and friends, giving her the reins to plan the activities at times. This will reaffirm your trust in her and build a stronger bond between you.

Remember that adventure may be the best way to engage in activities with your MY daughter. Encourage her to explore and try new activities, but make sure you teach her how to assess risk and make safe choices.

And finally, in this chapter, you learned that laughter is a powerful tool; one that is critical to getting on your child's level, showing your common interests, and bonding.

Find opportunities for humor and fun within your daily routine and make wonderful memories together. Create meaningful memories with your daughter, no matter if she is a CD or an MY, by participating in activities that she loves. These experiences will shape her childhood and are ultimately essential for her development and in building a strong parent-child bond.

Chapter Eight

Final Thoughts

Reflection on the Journey of Navigating Parenting with Varied Personality Types

As we come to the final chapter in this journey to provide 50 Ways to Love Your Daughter, it's essential to reflect on the path we've traveled, exploring the intricate dance of love and relationship with its different personality types—the Cave Dweller (CD), the Mountain Yeller (MY), and the Straddler, who possesses elements of both. Throughout this book, we have delved into the significance of understanding these personality types, how to communicate effectively, enhancing the bond you have with your child, balancing social lives between differing personalities, resonating emotionally with your daughter, and cultivating a lifelong bond and relationship with her.

Love truly is a dynamic and evolving force that connects you in ways you can never truly predict. Your daughter is a human being, and that human being is complex and beautiful.

Formulating and fostering a successful parent-child bond is not about finding the perfect formula or mastering a set of guidelines. Instead, it's about the dedication and effort you put into nurturing the unique love you share with those you love. Your daughter (whether a CD or an MY or somewhere in between) will appreciate the steps you have taken to communicate with and understand her in a way that no one else does. She will appreciate you making your relationship with her a priority.

The Importance of Continuous Effort and Growth in Maintaining a Healthy Relationship with Your Daughter

Your journey in this book has underscored the importance of continuous effort and growth in relationships. Love is not a static concept but instead is a force that thrives on the energy you invest in it. Every day, you have the opportunity to learn, adapt, and grow in your relationships. Your personalities evolve, and your needs change. It is forever important that you communicate with one another, focus on yourselves and those you love, and continue to maintain self-growth as well as growth within your relationships in order to be your happiest selves.

Embracing the Beauty of Parenting a CD or MY

Love is not a one-size-fits-all concept. It is as diverse and complex as the human beings who experience it. Through the pages of this book, we've explored the different personalities and even the personality in the middle. The fact that each personality type or individual may demonstrate their love or needs differently shows that there is no right or wrong way to love. It is important you celebrate these differences and embrace the individuality of your children.

Encouragement for Parents to Continually Love Their Daughter as She Evolves and Grows into a Woman While Using This Guide as a Tool for Strengthening Their Bond

The differences between personality types and each individual little girl are vast. By reading this guide, you should now be able to grapple with a sense of what it takes to develop patience, understanding, and empathy with your daughter, no matter her age.

Throughout *50 Ways to Love Your Daughter*, you have expanded your horizon and broadened your perspective and hopefully have obtained the tools and resources needed to learn from your daughter and the love you have for each other.

Embrace the differences you share with your daughter as well as your different emotional strengths. Learn from them and enhance your own emotional strengths as you do.

As we conclude this book, it is important for you, as your daughter's parent, to leave with the encouragement to continually evolve, adapt, and cherish the love you share for her.

It is quite easy to take someone for granted, especially after growing comfortable with them. Over time, it is natural to stop saying "Thank you" as often or to stop engaging emotionally. This leads to eventually devaluing one another and letting your relationship with your daughter slip between the cracks.

Never stop cherishing your little girl—no matter her age. Use the guidelines of this book to understand her needs and wants and how to continue to make her feel special and validated.

Start with yourself. Never stop learning about and working on yourself. It's often easy to focus on your children's shortcomings and overlook your own personal struggles. Hopefully, as you have learned more about your own motivations, as well as areas of strength and struggle, you have developed a new curiosity to discover even more.

When you hold your daughter to the same expectation that you hold yourself to, you realize it is quite natural to have shortcomings.

Make Time

Make time for your daughter, no matter what, and be consistent in that. It is quite easy—during transitioning into new seasons of life—to let your time with her slip away. Remember that time goes by a lot faster than you realize and she will be an adult before you know it. It's important that you have strong bonds with your children so that they want to remain in your lives consistently into adulthood.

Remember, your little girl may only be little for a short time, but you are ultimately hoping to go through this life *with her*. Make the time to be there for her to ensure that it's a strong and connected life together.

Moments of laughter and silliness or shared activity can quickly become your daughter's biggest and most precious memories. So, always make the time. No matter if she's a CD, an MY, or somewhere in between, she, like you, craves that precious quality time together.

Love, at its core, is all about being present in the moments you share. Make the time, cherish her, and embrace the ever-evolving journey of your relationship.

Show Your Love

Human touch and loving affection are needed at every stage of your life. It is critical that your child receives gentle, loving touch (hugs, kisses, etc.) from you several times throughout the day. Treat every interaction as an opportunity to connect with your daughter. Greet her with warm and positive expressions, give her eye contact, smile, and encourage honest interaction.

Set Boundaries, Rules, and Consequences

Remember that your daughter needs structure and guidance as she grows and learns about the world around her. Talk to your daughter about your expectations for her in a language that she understands. Also, explain what happens when she breaks the rules in place. Age-appropriate consequences are crucial.

Listen and Empathize

Connection starts with active listening. Acknowledge your daughter's feelings, show her that you understand, and reassure her that you are there to help her with whatever she may need. Try to see things from her perspective. By listening and empathizing with your daughter, you will begin to form mutual respect for one another.

Play Together

Play is so vital to your daughter's development. It is the light-hearted and fun tool through which she develops almost all of her initial skills, such as:

- Her language skills.
- Her ability to express emotions.
- Her creativity.
- Her social skills.

Additionally, play is just plain ol' fun. At the end of the day, it does not matter what you play. The key is to just enjoy your daughter and commit to giving her your complete and undivided attention.

Always Be Available and Distraction-Free

Grown-ups are often busy. Setting aside just ten minutes a day to talk to your daughter without distractions can make a huge difference in establishing good communication habits. Turn off the TV, put away your cell phone, and spend some quality time together. Your daughter needs to know that she is a priority.

Take the Lead

The most important relationship to your daughter is the one she develops with you—her parent or caregiver. Your daughter will learn about the world around her through positive attachments, and hopefully by reading this guide, you have gathered enough tools in your toolbox to truly become a positive and healthy connection. As your daughter grows and changes, she will continue to look at you to determine whether she is safe, secure, and loved. The relationship she has with you will be the foundation from which she will build all of her future relationships.

Ultimately, there is no secret handbook or guaranteed approach to get this parent-child relationship right, and you will likely find hardships along the way. However, if you keep working on improving your relationship with your daughter, she will surely blossom into a wonderful and well-balanced young woman.

Appendices

Self-Assessment Questionnaire: Determine If You're a CD, MY, or Straddler

In the quest for self-understanding, recognizing one's intrinsic personality traits plays a crucial role. This self-assessment questionnaire has been carefully designed to help you discern whether you align most closely with the introspective nature of a Cave Dweller (CD), the extroverted inclinations of a Mountain Yeller (MY), or the balanced characteristics of a Straddler. By reflecting on your behaviors, preferences, and reactions in various situations, this tool aims to provide insight into your predominant personality type. Approach each question with honesty and openness, and remember, there's no right or wrong answer—just a deeper understanding of your unique self waiting to be unveiled.

Personality Indicator #1

Circle one answer per question.

1. Have you ever walked in your sleep during your adult life?

   YES or NO

2. As a teenager, did you feel comfortable expressing your feelings to one or both of your parents?

   YES or NO

3. Do you have a tendency to look directly into a person's eyes when talking to them?

   YES or NO

4. Do you feel that most people, when you first meet them, are uncritical of your appearance?

   YES or NO

5. In a group situation with people you've just met, would you feel comfortable drawing attention to yourself by initiating a conversation?

   YES or NO

6. Do you feel comfortable holding hands or hugging someone you're in a relationship with in front of other people?

   YES or NO

7. When someone talks about feeling warm physically, do you begin to feel warm also?

   YES or NO

8. Do you tend to tune out when someone is talking to you because you're anxious to come up with your side of the story?

YES or NO

9. Do you feel that you learn better by seeing and/or reading than by hearing?

YES or NO

10. In a new class or company meeting, do you usually feel comfortable asking questions in front of the group?

YES or NO

11. When expressing your ideas, do you find it important to relate all the details leading up to the subject so the other person can understand it completely?

YES or NO

12. Do you enjoy relating to children?

YES or NO

13. Are you comfortable with your body movements when faced with unfamiliar people and circumstances?

YES or NO

14. Do you prefer reading fiction rather than nonfiction?

YES or NO

15. If you were to imagine sucking on a juicy lemon, would your mouth water?

    YES or NO

16. Do you feel comfortable receiving a compliment in front of other people?

    YES or NO

17. Do you feel that you're a good conversationalist?

    YES or NO

18. Do you feel comfortable when complimentary attention is drawn to your physical body?

    YES or NO

Personality Indicator #2

Circle one answer per question.

1. Have you ever awakened in the middle of the night and felt that you could not move your body and/or talk?

    YES or NO

2. As a child, did you feel you were more affected by your parents' tone of voice than by what they actually said?

    YES or NO

3. If someone you know talks about a fear that you've experienced before, do you have a tendency to re-experience that apprehension or fear?

YES or NO

4. After having an argument with someone, do you tend to dwell on what you could or should have said?

YES or NO

5. Do you tend to occasionally tune out when someone is talking to you and, therefore, don't hear what's being said because your mind drifts to something totally unrelated?

YES or NO

6. Do you sometimes desire to be complimented for a job well done but feel embarrassed or uncomfortable when complemented?

YES or NO

7. Do you often fear not being able to carry on a conversation with someone you've just met?

YES or NO

8. Do you feel self-conscious when attention is drawn to your physical body or appearance?

YES or NO

9. If you had a choice, would you rather avoid being around

children most of the time?

YES or NO

10. Do you feel uptight in body movements, especially when faced with unfamiliar people or circumstances?

YES or NO

11. Do you prefer reading nonfiction rather than fiction?

YES or NO

12. If someone describes a very bitter taste, do you have difficulty experiencing the physical feeling of that bitter taste?

YES or NO

13. Do you generally feel that you see yourself less favorably than others see you?

YES or NO

14. Do you tend to feel awkward or self-conscious holding hands and/or kissing someone you're in a relationship with in front of other people?

YES or NO

15. In a new lecture or company meeting, do you usually feel uncomfortable asking questions in front of the group?

YES or NO

16. Do you feel uneasy if someone you've just met looks you directly in the eyes when talking to you, especially if the conversation is about you?

    YES or NO

17. In a group situation with people you've just met, would you feel uncomfortable drawing attention to yourself by initiating a conversation?

    YES or NO

18. If you're in a relationship or are very close to someone, do you find it difficult or embarrassing to verbalize your love for them?

    YES or NO

Personality Indicator Scores

Personality Indicator #1

- Give yourself 10 points for every "yes" answer for questions 1 and 2.

- Give yourself 5 points for every answer for questions 3–18.

- Write the total number at the top of the #1 questionnaire.

Personality Indicator #2

- Give yourself 10 points for every yes answer for questions 1 and 2.

- Give yourself 5 points for every answer for questions 3–18.

- Write the total number at the top of the #2 questionnaire.

- Combine the total from Personality Indicators 1 and 2.

Using the Scoring Chart

On the scoring chart, look up the combined score of Personality Indicator 1 and 2 on the HORIZONTAL axis of the chart and circle the number.

- Take the total score of Personality Indicator #1, locate it on the VERTICAL axis of the chart, and circle the number.

- Draw a horizontal line across the page from the Personality Indicator 1 score, then draw a vertical line down from the combined score.

- The number in the box where the two lines intersect represents your true, adjusted percentage Personality Indicator.

- Scores 61 and higher indicate a Mountain Yeller personality type.

- Scores 45 and lower indicate a Cave Dweller personality type.

- Scores 47–56 indicate a Straddler personality type.

Cave Dweller Tendencies

- Reserved
- Head ruled
- Controlling
- Wants space and security
- Prefers socializing one-on-one
- Singular focus
- Thinks before reacting
- Prefers showing affection privately
- Distrusts flattery
- Enjoys working alone
- Enjoys individual activities
- Wants alone time
- Dresses for comfort
- Decides after thinking about it
- Speaks literally—to the point
- Infers from what others say
- Feels emotional pain in the mind
- Fears loss of security

Cave Dweller Priorities

- Career/Financial Security
- Hobbies/Children
- Relationships/Family
- Sex/Lovers

Mountain Yeller Tendencies

- Outgoing
- Heart ruled
- Dominating
- Wants connection and touch
- Enjoys socializing in groups
- Moving focus
- Reacts spontaneously
- Comfortable with affection anytime
- Likes reassurance and compliments
- Enjoys working with people
- Enjoys team activities
- Wants to be together as much as possible

- Decides in the moment

- Speaks inferentially—adds story

- Takes literally what others say

- Feels emotional pain in body and mind

- Fears rejection

Mountain Yeller Priorities

- Relationships/Sex

- Family/Children

- Friends/Hobbies

- Career/Financial security

COMBINED SCORE #1 AND #2

SCORE #1	50	55	60	65	70	75	80	85	90	95	100	105	110	115	120	125	130	135	140	145	150	155	160	165	170	175	180	185	190	195	200
100											100	95	91	87	83	80	77	74	71	69	67	65	63	61	59	57	56	54	53	51	50
95										100	96	90	86	83	79	76	73	70	68	66	63	61	59	58	56	54	53	51	50	49	48
90									100	95	90	86	82	78	75	72	69	67	64	62	60	58	56	55	53	51	50	49	47	46	45
85								100	94	89	85	81	77	74	71	68	66	63	61	59	57	56	53	52	50	49	47	46	45	44	43
80							100	94	89	84	80	76	73	70	67	64	62	59	57	55	53	52	50	48	47	46	44	43	42	41	40
75						100	94	88	83	79	75	71	68	65	63	60	58	56	54	52	50	48	47	46	44	43	42	41	39	38	38
70					100	93	88	82	78	74	70	67	64	61	58	56	54	52	50	48	47	45	44	43	42	41	40	39	38	37	36
65				100	93	87	81	76	72	68	65	62	59	57	54	52	50	48	46	45	43	42	41	39	38	37	36	35	34	33	33
60			100	92	86	80	75	71	67	63	60	57	55	52	50	48	46	44	43	41	40	39	38	36	35	34	33	32	32	31	30
55		100	92	85	79	73	69	65	61	58	55	52	50	48	46	44	42	41	39	38	37	35	34	33	32	31	31	30	29	28	28
50	100	91	83	77	71	67	63	59	56	53	50	48	45	43	42	40	38	37	36	34	33	32	31	30	29	29	28	27	26	26	25
45	90	82	75	69	64	60	56	53	50	47	45	43	41	39	38	36	35	33	32	31	30	29	28	27	26	26	25	24	23	23	
40	80	73	67	62	57	53	50	47	44	42	40	38	36	35	33	32	31	30	29	28	27	26	25	24	24	23	22	22	21	21	20
35	70	64	58	54	50	47	44	41	39	37	35	33	32	30	29	28	27	26	25	24	23	23	22	21	21	20	19	19	18	18	18
30	60	55	50	46	43	40	38	35	33	32	30	29	27	26	25	24	23	22	21	21	20	19	19	18	18	17	17	16	16	15	15
25	50	46	42	38	36	33	31	29	28	26	25	24	23	22	21	20	19	19	18	17	17	16	16	15	15	14	14	14	13	13	13
20	40	36	33	31	29	27	25	24	22	21	20	19	18	17	17	16	15	15	14	14	13	13	12	12	11	11	11	11	10	10	
15	30	27	25	23	21	20	19	18	17	16	15	14	14	13	13	12	12	11	11	10	10	10	9	9	9	8	8	8	8		
10	20	18	17	15	14	13	13	12	11	11	10	10	9	9	8	8	8	7	7	7	6	6	6	6	6	5	5	5	5		
5	10	9	8	8	7	7	6	6	6	5	5	5	5	4	4	4	4	4	3	3	3	3	3	3	3	3	3	3	3		
0	0	0	0	0	0	0	0	0	0	0	0	0	0	0	0	0	0	0	0	0	0	0	0	0	0	0	0	0	0	0	0

About the Author

Dr. Cline lives with her husband, two daughters, two German Shepherds, and two Yorkies in the hills of North Carolina. Her expertise in relationship building has offered her the opportunity to travel around the world as a keynote speaker and international workshop facilitator.

www.ingramcontent.com/pod-product-compliance
Lightning Source LLC
Chambersburg PA
CBHW070107080526
44586CB00013B/1216